What Rea

"The material in this handbook helped me clarify my own vision and open myself to someone who could share that vision and help bring it to life. I found that person in an amazingly short period of time."

Mark Vanderpool
Participant,
Finding Your Soul Mate Workshop

"Inspirational ... provides insights on how to have what we want and not settle for less, in all our relationships."

Angeles Arrien, Ph.D.,
Author of The Four-Fold Way and The Nine Muses

"I wish I had found Evelyn Rice's Finding Your Soul Mate™ Handbook forty, thirty, or even twenty years ago. I heartily recommend this book to anyone, singles or couples, who want to keep their lives on the high path."

Dr. Helen Andrews
Certified Imago relationship therapist

"Going beyond theory, Evelyn presents an integrated approach to relationship based on her own experience of how to blend both the spiritual and practical."

Brian Ziegler,
Retail executive

What participants of Evelyn K. Rice's Finding Your Soul Mate™ Workshop say about its impact on their lives

"The resources Evelyn provided have helped me recognize and embrace the opportunity at hand. I am thankful every day for the subtle but profound changes I have experienced, and continue to experience, since I was exposed to this material."

"I now know there is no need for me to think I have to compromise anything I want in a long-term relationship.... Thanks for showing me what's possible."

"I walked away saying this was by far the most powerful relationship workshop I have ever attended. It was awesome! I definitely could have used the knowledge I gained a long time ago, and so could someone else I 'used' to know."

"As a survivor of domestic violence, I now work for a battered women's shelter. Your material provided answers in a way I had never seen before. Many will benefit from this work!"

"You gave me the push I needed to let go of the past and create a plan of action for a much happier and satisfying future with my wife."

FINDING
YOUR SOUL MATE™
HANDBOOK

The Journey of
Attracting and Creating
Loving and Successful Relationships

by

Evelyn K. Rice

Published by

Rice & Associates, Inc.

P.O. Box 38263

Greensboro, NC 27438

(336) 370-1555

email: ekrice@riceassociates.com

www.riceassociates.com

ISBN   0-9711207-0-6

Library of Congress Control Number: 2001118646

Rice, Evelyn K. (1958-) Finding Your Soul Mate™ Handbook: The Journey of Attracting and Creating Loving and Successful Relationships / Evelyn K. Rice

1. Love   2. Interpersonal Relationships   3. Marriage   4.Intimacy (Psychology)   5. Spirituality

Printed in the U.S.A.

Cover art and book design

Gemini Group, Greensboro, NC 27401

About the people in this book:

The stories involving participants in my workshops are real, but their names are not. I have changed the names of all involved to protect their privacy.

DEDICATION

*For Chris and Nancy, who walk beside me
in unconditional love.*

ACKNOWLEDGMENTS

I owe a great debt to some very dear friends who encouraged and supported me, told me "the absolute truth," and pushed me to get this work out into the world. Thank you Beverly Royston, Carol Rhodes, Pat Henry, Marguerite Lawn, Sunya Webber, Cindy Blevins, Troy Ann Williams, Lisa Whicker, Joy Nelson, Adria Zimmerman, and Becky Lankford for helping me get this miraculous undertaking underway.

A special acknowledgment also to Linda Rachel, Pam Pauley, and Bill Turner of the Wisdom Network for their consistent support and belief in my potential. Also to Angeles Arrien, Betty Work, and David Arneke for their generous contribution to this work. And with deep gratitude to the late Dr. Jim Farr, for his commitment to helping me truly understand and integrate the principles of self-awareness.

With heartfelt thankfulness to Rebekah Dunlap and Robert E. Krumroy whose foundational contribution make this book possible.

And grateful thanks to all of my friends, clients, and family members whose experiences made this work real to me in my own life.

Much love to you all.

Evelyn K. Rice

CONTENTS

THE JOURNEY BEGINS

"For one human being to love another;
that is perhaps the most difficult task of all ...,
the work for which all other work is but preparation.
It is a high inducement to the individual to ripen ...
a great exacting claim upon us,
something that chooses us out
and calls us to vast things."

Rainer Maria Rilke

My feet were aching. I was exhausted and hungry. Dragging a laden luggage cart behind me through the Madison, Wisconsin, airport, the only thing I cared about was finding a place to sit until my plane was ready to board.

I plopped down beside an elderly gentleman and gave him a sideways glance. His face resonated with deep calm and inner peace, and somehow he reminded me of another time, another place, maybe someone I had once known. Déjà vu? Who knows?

Resting my tired head on my hands, I reflected on the week I had just spent working with a group of bankers on improving their communications skills. The training program had required tremendous time, energy, and commitment. And at the same time I was privately struggling with a major decision that would change the course of my life.

Back home was a man I loved dearly. But the two years we had been together required so much effort and created such intense emotional highs and lows that I felt drained all the time. Love wasn't meant to be like this — surely. I'd always believed that truly deep love between two people was like a sanctuary — a place where you felt protected, respected, comforted, and cherished.

During my week in Madison, I had prayed and meditated several times a day, searching for guidance. I was heartsick. How could you love someone so much, but have to struggle all the time to make it work?

After four days, the answer came as a definite, yet peaceful knowing. *End the relationship!* I knew it was right. Something deep inside me had finally spoken clearly. Or maybe for the first time I had decided to listen and not let fear overshadow what I needed to hear. From that moment, I knew I would be all right. The future could and would hold wonderful experiences, if only I listened to my heart's inner guidance.

"You're going to India, aren't you?"

Deep in thought, I nearly jumped out of my skin. The white-haired gentleman at my side was talking to me! And he was right! I was going to India!

But how could a total stranger at an airport in Wisconsin possibly know that? And he knew a great deal more. "You're going to certain special places during your trip, aren't you?" he informed me, naming the sites I planned to visit.

More than a little nervous, I wanted to get up and move. But something gripped my soul and froze me to the seat. My thoughts tumbled. Who was this man? How did he know so much about me? *"How did you know that?"* I finally demanded.

And then he shocked me even more. "I am supposed to share something very important with you," he said with a smile. "You won't understand why I am sharing this with you today, but one day you will."

He introduced himself as Jerry, and he began telling me about the three foundational keys a Soul Mate relationship is built on. An hour flew by, and we continued talking during the two-hour flight to Chicago. Rather, he talked and I tried to absorb it all.

At the Chicago airport, we parted; and as he was walking away, he turned a final time and said to me, "What you do with this information is your choice. If you use it, it will serve you well."

Standing there in that concourse, jostled on all sides by hurrying travelers, I reflected on this amazing encounter. I knew that meeting Jerry was no accident. He was there for *me.*

And I also reflected on what this remarkable stranger had said about choices. I knew I had a choice to make at home — a sad and painful choice, but a necessary one. I would end a turbulent relationship and have the courage to face a different kind of future.

On that day, I made a pact to never again settle for anything less than a Soul Mate relationship. And I embarked on an exciting journey of understanding about what love really is.

SOUL MATE LOVE

...So much more than most imagine.
An emotion that stirs the deepest of one's soul.

Like a fire that wraps her arms
around one's inner being.
A passion, which embraces the memories of yesterday
and the anticipation for one's tomorrows.

What unfathomable joy to experience its fullness
and to be captured by love's soft embrace.

A Mystery...waiting to unfold.
A journey that is yours, if
...you are ready to begin.

Robert Krumroy

WHAT IS A SOUL MATE RELATIONSHIP?

Soul Mate relationships are created when two individuals consciously choose to come together for the opportunity to experience joy and to share in each other's growth – emotionally, mentally, physically, and spiritually.

These relationships are typically passionate, harmonious, and productive. When challenging times arise, Soul Mates know that to maintain a healthy relationship, they must continue to make *conscious* choices. Successful relationships are all about choices – choices that are made with awareness, that are compassionately proactive rather than sternly reactive. The quality of the relationship is always determined by each individual's willingness to take responsibility for his or her own history. It is a union of two people contributing positively to the relationship and maintaining a willingness to honor each other in the relationship journey.

In healthy and well-balanced relationships, each person takes one hundred percent responsibility for his or her life and for the results he or she creates for themselves and the relationship. In a

Soul Mate relationship, you aren't dependent on your partner to "make" you feel one way or another or to solve your problems. Soul Mates take responsibility for themselves. They acknowledge that their partners are gifts to help them see their own areas for growth and to increase their understanding of themselves.

One of the myths about Soul Mates is, *"If I find my Soul Mate, all my relationship challenges will dissolve."* If you're looking for a relationship that will solve all your problems, you're inevitably going to be disappointed. The Soul Mate relationship is not about perfection. No one is perfect.

This myth of the perfect relationship has contributed to many a person's frustration and loss of hope in relationships. Even if we have a potentially great relationship that we feel was destined to be, when we don't understand the physical, mental, and emotional components that drive us, we are like ships without rudders or airplanes without navigators. We can unwittingly sabotage a potentially healthy and satisfying Soul Mate relationship. If we are to achieve and maintain a *living* connection with our intimate partner, it is imperative that we free ourselves from wishful, unrealistic fantasies. We can take the personal blinders from our eyes and develop the full range of our abilities, sensitivities, powers, and depths as human beings.

Consciousness is the first step toward achieving that goal. The second step is *commitment.*

Creating a Soul Mate relationship isn't easy. It doesn't just "happen." That's why we talk of *creating* this relationship. It requires a commitment to growth, to reality, and to facing some hard truths about ourselves. Taking off those blinders reveals not only our potential but also our fears and weaknesses. Overcoming these fears and weaknesses is hard work. It requires a strong commitment.

Like the Soul Mate relationship itself, commitment doesn't just happen. The source of commitment is *courage*. Creating a Soul Mate relationship isn't to be entered into lightly. Without courage, we are likely to turn away from our fears. We will deny our weaknesses. We will ignore the disappointments, the anger, and the hurt that are in our past. And by not facing the fears, the weaknesses, and the pain that we all have, we allow them to drive our life. We allow them to dictate and destroy our relationships. We allow them to keep us from our Soul Mates.

Courage allows us to make the commitment. The commitment allows us to make conscious choices. The conscious choices allow us to overcome the problems that have sabotaged our past relationships. Together, they can move us to take the step – the frightening, thrilling step – to seek out and attract a Soul Mate relationship.

Any single step can open the door to unexpected and phenomenal opportunities. We can change our personal visions so that we can see life working *for* us rather than *against* us. It has been said that the only thing that can limit the fulfillment of our desires is our own lack of understanding and our failure to go forward in truth. We can stand on the edge of opportunity and wish, or we can jump straight into the heart of the matter. What is priority number one? Honesty! Being honest with yourself first, and then with others.

HOW TO GET THE MOST OUT OF THIS BOOK

The powerful and tremendous meaning of creating a Soul Mate relationship is described fully in the pages of this handbook. This step-by-step, *practical* guide shows you not only how to attract a Soul Mate, but also how to move an existing relationship closer to the fulfilling Soul Mate relationship you desire and which life offers as a precious gift. Diligently completing every exercise and practicing the strategies and skills presented here will make you aware of how you're contributing to your goals – as well as how you're possibly getting in your own way!

Keep this book in a handy place. Thoroughly study the methods and procedures described. Underline the points that are important to you. Apply the ideas to your daily life. List your goals and desires, and keep a journal of your progress. Let the meaning of the words flow over your soul, opening new avenues of awareness as you attune your mind to the rhythm of a Soul Mate relationship.

I highly recommend you create a Soul Mate Journal to record notes on what you read and what is happening in your life.

Writing encourages you to focus your thoughts and, more precisely, to identify your feelings. Your thoughts and feelings are a vitally important part of your life. The more clarity and understanding you have in these areas, the richer your experiences can be.

Make a list of questions that come to mind as you work with this material. Every question takes us on a journey! Make a note of "first responses" that occur to you when you ask the questions. Look more deeply into the theme of your questions and note this information in your Soul Mate Journal. Your journal will be an excellent tool for documenting the progress and growth you're experiencing. You'll develop a clearer awareness about who you are, where you are in your life now, and where you're choosing to go.

Completing the exercises in this book and taking the necessary steps to integrate the material into your experience will require patience and diligence. It's worth it!

THE BITS AND PIECES EXERCISE

This is your first exercise. Don't skip it! Don't skip any! All of them will deepen and expand your awareness, and all of them will build the highway to a desirable Soul Mate relationship.

Goal: To consciously acknowledge relationships in your life that possess the qualities and components of a successful and satisfying relationship.

Practice: Start a Soul Mate Journal. Notice relationships around you that give a sense of well-being, happiness, and joy. Write down the behaviors and characteristics of the healthy, happy relationships you observe. Do this for one week.

Result: This exercise focuses your attention on those qualities and traits you desire for yourself, as well as those you want to create in your relationships.

"The real voyage of discovery
consists not in seeking new landscapes,
but in having new eyes."
Marcel Proust

PART I

SHARED REALITY

The First Foundational Key

"If you don't know where you're going,
any road will get you there then."

Cheshire Cat,

Alice's Adventures in Wonderland

CHAPTER ONE

THE POWER OF PURPOSE

"Nothing contributes so much to tranquilize the mind
as a steady purpose – a point on which
the soul may fix its intellectual eye."
Mary Shelley

"Where there is no vision, the people perish."
Ancient proverb

Everyone needs dreams and goals – a sense of purpose – to live life fully. If you don't have specific goals in mind or don't know where you want to go, you may end up in places – *and with people* – not of your own choosing.

Establishing goals, and guidelines on how to achieve them, will help keep you focused and energized. It also will make your life's journey more interesting, rewarding, and successful. As someone once said: "All the things you are seeking are perfectly natural and are seeking you!"

Shared Reality

"Well begun is half done."

Aristotle

The first foundational key for creating or drawing a Soul Mate relationship into your life is Shared Reality. What we mean by Shared Reality is an understanding that when two people have goals and values that align with each other, they increase their chances for experiencing a reality of support and trust. It holds true in all areas of our lives.

Shared Reality also exists when two people *consciously* create a shared space for relating to each other — acknowledging, respecting, and honoring each other's personal growth, goals, and dreams. Before you can experience Shared Reality, however, you have to understand your reality — your own growth, goals, and dreams.

Let's take a look now at the two initial steps that lay the foundation for Shared Reality with another person. The first is **Identifying Your Purpose**; the second is **Identifying Your Feelings**.

Identifying Purpose

"First ponder, then dare!"

Helmuth von Moltke

Creating Shared Reality with another begins with identifying your reasons for wanting to be part of a Soul Mate relationship.

It will require diligent soul-searching, a heightened *awareness* of yourself and everything around you.

Awareness is one of the most basic qualities for enhancing your life. The more awareness you possess, the more skilled you will be at handling whatever arises. It's also one of the most essential and powerful resources you can have for effecting change, understanding and pursuing your true desires, and working through challenges.

By identifying your purpose, you chart a course for the future based on what's most important for you to achieve or experience in a relationship. Your answers to these two self-directed questions will help clarify how you define your purpose at this point in your life. In fact, they're questions that need to be asked periodically as you grow and redefine your purpose.

Question 1:

"If I had only six months to live, what would I want my life to represent in the area of relationships?"

Question 2:

"What impact would I like to make in this life for myself and others?"

You may end up with one overriding purpose for your life in general, plus different purposes that relate to work, relationships, and other areas of your life. Just be sure they all complement your overall life purpose and contain no contradictions. This way, you are cultivating harmony.

People who don't establish a purpose for the relationships in their lives inevitably find themselves as lost as Alice in Wonderland.

> "*Alice was walking down a road one day when she came to a huge fork in the middle of the road. Now, off of this fork in the road were many roads going in many different directions. In the middle of this fork in the road stood a huge tree with a large trunk and huge limbs with beautiful green leaves. When Alice stopped at the bottom of this tree, she happened to look up and there in the tree sat a Cheshire Cat with huge green eyes looking down at her. Alice looked up and said, 'Cheshire Cat, which one of these many roads should I take?' The Cheshire Cat said, 'Alice, which way do you want to go?' She said, 'I don't know.' He said, 'If you don't know where you're going, any road will get you there then.'*"
>
> (*from* Lewis Carroll's *Alice's Adventures in Wonderland*)

Are you an Alice? If you don't know what direction you want to take in a relationship or what your ultimate goals are, you are highly likely to wind up somewhere you never intended to be. Before taking off on your journey, it's critical to first understand your purpose for going.

Clarifying Purpose

> "Our aspirations are our possibilities."
>
> *Samuel Johnson*

The word "relationship" should give you pause for thought. It points to what may be humankind's greatest challenge: the need to awaken, each in our own way, to the greater possibilities of shared communication and communion. It represents one of life's deep urges to move forward in a particular way.

When we're drawn by this sense of forward momentum, there's an unmistakable stream of vitality flowing through us. Unfortunately, we're often off-balance with this force moving deep within. The 13th-century Sufi poet Rumi, whose writings about the deep longings of the human heart resonate strongly even today, described it vividly: *"We who are blind think our horse is lost, yet all the while he is sweeping us onward like the wind."* Let us not continue to be unconsciously asleep in the saddle!

Stop now and ask yourself these four key questions:

- *Am I willing to make a commitment to movement and change?*
- *Am I willing to be open to learn exactly where I personally most need to grow?*
- *Am I willing to make honest, direct contact with life?*
- *Am I willing to connect more deeply, not with just my partner but with my own personal awareness as well?*

These are not questions to be taken lightly. Producing absolutely honest answers will require you to overcome inertia, counter-productive habits, and memories of past mistakes. You'll have to confront fear of failure ... and maybe even fear of success. But do it you must! This is a test of your commitment and courage. How well you face these questions will have a huge impact on your ability to create a Soul Mate relationship.

Using the worksheet on the following page, put in writing why you want to be in a Soul Mate relationship. You may think — well, isn't it obvious? You may surprise yourself. In any event, putting your thoughts in writing will send a message to yourself that this desire is important enough to document!

Write your first thoughts. You are making a definite commitment *now* — a commitment to what you want, a commitment to an intensified relationship of happiness and fulfillment. Write what your thoughts are *now*. As you progress on your journey, you can always return and make changes as you further clarify your purpose.

My purpose for being in a Soul Mate relationship is

_____

_____

_____

_____

_____

_____

_____

_____

_____

_____

Here's what I wrote for myself:

"My purpose for being in a Soul Mate relationship is to share with another a journey of mental, spiritual, physical, and emotional growth, full of light, love, and joy."

Don't concern yourself with "getting it right." As Oprah Winfrey tells her audience, "We are people in process." Start with where you are now. As you do your Soul Mate work, you'll begin clarifying your purpose as you go. The important thing is to start somewhere. *Accept* where you are today — don't fight it. It's hard to get where you want to **go** if you don't know exactly where you're starting **from**.

By writing down your initial thoughts of what your purpose is, you have begun the journey of finding your Soul Mate. Congratulations! You have taken the first step.

When we welcome the growth opportunities that a clear purpose provides, a relationship becomes a powerful and dynamic force in our overall development. And the beautiful thing is that the tools presented in this handbook apply equally well to *all* relationships: job, employer, family, friends, and acquaintances. So if you skipped the first brief writing assignment, please go back and do it now. It's your first step toward an exciting journey.

Identifying Your Feelings

So many times when setting goals for our lives, we overlook the power of our feelings. Think of a few memories from your past and note the "labels" you've attached to each of them. It's typical for human beings to label memories as good, bad, pleasant, or unpleasant. We base conclusions about these memories on how we recall feeling about the experience.

In this, the second step for laying the foundation for Shared Reality with another person, you will identify the **feelings** you want to experience in a Soul Mate relationship. This exercise will put your emotions and desires into powerful alignment.

As always, you must be honest with yourself and search the deep corners of your mind to determine the strength and effectiveness of your feelings. Now, add a second part to your **Purpose Statement:**

My purpose for being in a Soul Mate relationship is

_____

_____

_____

_____

_____

_____

_____

so I may experience: (feelings): _____

_____

_____

_____

_____

Identifying both your **purpose** and the **feelings** you desire in a Soul Mate relationship will help you stay on track with your dreams and goals. Your written, clarified **Purpose and Feeling Statement** can now act as a guidepost. It will allow you to clearly see your outer world and then determine whether it's in alignment with your inner desires and dreams. If that alignment is lacking, it's time to reassess the words, thoughts, and actions that may be stopping you from achieving your desired growth and objectives.

Dreaming Big

Jim came to one of my workshops not long after the demise of what he described as a "wonderful" eight-year relationship. He and Stella had cared deeply for each other, he said, but didn't seem to be anything close to being Soul Mates. They had very few interests in common. Jim's idea of a Soul Mate was someone who dreamed big, sought adventure, and loved sharing stimulating ideas. This was definitely not Stella. Their purposes in life didn't seem to mesh in any way. Now, as he geared up to seek a new companion, he had a question: "Should I narrow the search for my Soul Mate based on whether she shares my interests?"

Jim's quandary underlines the importance of *first* identifying your purpose before questing after a relationship. I responded by reminding him that each person has to decide what specific qualities are required to make a good match. Some people are very undemanding — affection and a few common interests are enough. Others — like Jim — want it all! For them, settling for less ultimately leads to unhappiness and the end of the relationship.

Each of us has to decide what we really want from a relationship and make sure it doesn't feel like a compromise with our purpose. Finding a partner who's mentally, physically, emotionally, and spiritually compatible with you can be a big help in creating the foundation for a long-term relationship that's full of life and passion.

> "Creativity requires the harnessing of feelings
> as well as thinking."
> *George Vaillant*

NOTES:

Overview of Key Concepts and Ideas

- It's important to be clear about your purpose for being in a Soul Mate relationship.
- Identifying the feelings and emotions you want to experience in a Soul Mate relationship is your daily guidepost to measuring your alignment with your goals.
- Shared Reality is a foundation of the Soul Mate relationship. It occurs when two individuals have goals and values that are conscious and align with each other, yet provide mutual support to honor each other's personal growth, goals, and dreams.

Three-Step Action Plan

1. Identify and write down your purpose for being in a Soul Mate relationship.
2. Identify and write down the feelings you wish to experience in this relationship.
3. Notice the qualities of relationships around you that mirror what you desire.

CHAPTER TWO

CREATING DESIRES THROUGH INTENTION

"Nothing happens unless first a dream."
Carl Sandberg

Once you have established your purpose for being in a Soul Mate relationship and identified the primary emotions you wish to experience, it's time to begin designing what your *"ideal Soul Mate relationship"* would look like. Base your design on an understanding of how sharing your life with this person would help you achieve your purpose in life.

Identifying the specific qualities you desire in a Soul Mate is a crucial first step in this process. Never approach a new relationship with an attitude of "I hope they choose me." **Know** in advance what you want in a relationship and use those criteria to determine if this person fills the bill. It's definitely your best chance for finding a partner whose objectives are in alignment with yours, someone with strong potential to eventually walk beside you as friend, lover, and ally.

You already possess the three vital elements for achieving your goals – your **spiritual** qualities, your **mental/emotional** qualities, and your **physical** qualities. They're with you wherever you may be and in whatever activities you may participate.

By using the *"Designing Your Own Soul Mate"* tool in this book, you will be able to identify *specifically* the kind of person who would fulfill your dreams – spiritually, mentally/emotionally, and physically. In so doing, you create a "sticky note" for your mental computer that serves as a reminder as you go through your day.

Knowing the **facts** of what you want can bring you closer to achieving your goals. You will filter out the expectations and demands of others. You make it very clear about what you want, dream, and desire. Then as you meet people, you will have an invaluable tool to help determine whether they are on a compatible track.

In today's busy world, we're so bombarded with data and information that it's easy to get distracted from our goals. Your **Soul Mate Design** will help keep you aware of important possibilities in your surroundings. As someone said, "Opportunities aren't as rare as your ability to see them."

By taking the time to clarify what your desires are, you won't be wasting time wandering down wrong paths. Your path will lead to many opportunities and the knowledge that your Soul Mate is waiting for you along the way.

Now, let's take a closer look at the three attributes that determine your ability to achieve your goals.

Spiritual Qualities

Spiritual qualities are your base foundation. They support your purpose in life. Yogi Ramacharaka touched on them in his book *The Life beyond Death.*

"There are three great truths which are absolute, and which cannot be lost, but yet remain silent for lack of speech. (1) The soul of man is immortal, and its future is the future of a thing whose growth and splendor have no limit. (2) The principle which gives life dwells in us, and without us; is undying and eternally beneficial; is not heard, or seen, or felt, but is perceived by the one who desires perception. (3) Each person is his own absolute law-giver; the dispenser of glory or gloom to himself, the one who decrees his life, his reward, his punishment. These truths are as great as life itself, are as simple as the most simple mind ... Feed the hunger with them."

The bottom line is – you are a magnificent spiritual being! Spiritual qualities that will support your quest for a Soul Mate relationship include a loving and compassionate attitude toward others, finding quiet time each day for meditation or prayer, and an interest in spiritual growth and education.

Mental/Emotional Qualities

Mental/emotional qualities include your temperament, your personality, how you interact with others – your overall attitude toward life. If you continue putting forth your best effort while focusing on your own loving intentions in all circumstances — your highest thoughts every day — your energy will become a radiant positive magnet. If you remain poised and balanced, realizing the importance of being compassionate and generous in all situations and with everybody you meet — not just potential Soul Mates — your personality will blossom.

All too often, I've heard people say they "don't feel like" being a loving person. "I'm just not motivated to extend myself," they admit. What I say is: Whether you **feel like** acting loving or not doesn't really matter. You just need to **do** it! Feelings rarely precede action. Put forth an effort when you don't feel like it, and the feelings and motivation will follow.

In truth, success in any area of life is a matter of doing what is required whether you feel like it or not. Don't wait until the mood strikes you. **Communicate** your loving intentions. Your potential Soul Mate relationship deserves no less.

Physical Qualities

At times it seems the entire world has looked in the mirror and come away disgruntled. *Too tall, too short, too fat, bad skin, crooked teeth, bad hair.* Sometimes the whole lot! How you look and how you feel about your physical presence can powerfully affect your outlook toward your goals. The 19th-century Persian sage 'Abdu'l-Bahá, who spent forty years in a Turkish prison, remarked: "There is no prison save that of self." Enough said!

This is What I Want!

Below you will find a sample chart for listing **On Purpose Goals** — the initial step for *"Designing Your Own Soul Mate"* from the spiritual, mental/emotional, and physical perspectives.

On the chart I completed for myself, I identified twenty-seven desired qualities for my Soul Mate. Let me tell you what happened next.

On Purpose Goals
Spiritual
Mental/Emotional
Physical

After meeting Jerry (the gentleman in the Wisconsin airport) and making a commitment to never settle for less than exactly what I wanted, I began exploring the three key points and what they meant to me. I began attending every workshop I could on how to become a healthier person.

A few months into this journey, my friend Martin called to invite me to his wedding. He added an intriguing inducement: "I have found the man of your dreams. Come to the wedding, and you will meet him."

I arrived at the wedding early, and so did Chris, the pre-advertised "man of my dreams." So far so good — I felt an instant rapport with him. We chattered away like old friends, so engrossed with each other, in fact, that we missed the start of the wedding.

Chris was coming out of a long-term relationship, and I knew that getting involved with him at that point was not a good choice. We agreed to keep in touch, hugged goodbye ... *and my heart leaped!* I felt a great attraction to this man, and it wasn't just physical. Could he be the one? I wanted to stay, go, hide, pursue. I didn't know what I wanted to do! I only knew that something was quite different.

Over the next two months Chris and I talked on the phone every week. I sensed a strong connection, yet kept reminding myself that he had to do his healing and closure work around his former marriage, which had just recently dissolved. I didn't want to be his "transformational healing object," someone who assists another person through the healing and pain of a breakup. Relationships that start under those circumstances rarely work out. The "healed" person eventually moves on, leaving behind the person who became associated with the closure of the "old" relationship.

Being so very attracted to Chris — his intellect, his passion for life — made the next few months challenging. But I held to my convictions, deciding to risk short-term pain for long-term gain. I knew there was something between us that was worth the wait. My mind and body kept coaxing, "Go for it!" but my heart and soul counseled, "Wait!" I waited, and used the time to discover how well Chris aligned with my written qualities for a Soul Mate.

In May, Chris and I shared our feelings about our mutual attraction and decided to continue being great friends as he worked through the closure of his marriage.

In September, I left for my long-planned tour of India. I would be gone a month. And as I left Chris standing at the airport at Charlotte, North Carolina, I felt incredible joy and contentment. I had stayed true to my goal of waiting until this man was available one hundred percent before getting into a committed, intimate relationship with him. Chris still had some healing to complete, and we both honored and respected that personal journey while maintaining our friendship.

Three weeks later, I was in the mountains of Nepal when the phone rang in my hotel room. It was Chris, and he began to tell me how much I meant to him, how much he cared for me. He said he had taken care of the personal challenges he had been working on. He wanted to know if I would be interested in taking the next step in our relationship when I came home. "Yes," I said in my calmest voice. My girlfriends who had accompanied me to India hung on every word. "What did he say, what did he say?" they demanded as I hung up the phone. And finally I couldn't hold back my elation. I jumped up and down on the bed, roaring, *"Yes! Yes! Yes!"*

When Chris and I began dating, I discovered that he possessed twenty-five of the twenty-seven qualities on my Designing Your

Own Soul Mate list. That was an incredible match! The two qualities that didn't match were my stylized idea of a dreamboat: 6-feet-2 with eyes of blue. What I found instead was a wonderful soul who is 5-feet-10 with eyes of gorgeous brown. And I made the discovery that those original physical descriptions didn't matter to me in the least.

A Design of Your Own

Now its your turn to *"Design Your Own Soul Mate"*. Not withstanding minor readjustments you might make later, be as detailed and specific as possible when listing the qualities you desire in a Soul Mate. List as least five in each category when filling out the worksheets on the following pages. Think about what qualities in another person are important to you and take as much time as you need to clarify your desires.

Feel the energy of the words you write. Feel the excitement of being the actual designer of your own Soul Mate. Your mind is a fantastic mental magnet. Feel the power of universal love pulsing through the qualities you list. Be specific, then allow yourself to be open and receptive to the wondrous miracles and surprises the universe may have in store for you. "This, or something better!" playwright Somerset Maugham said. "It's a funny thing about life; if you refuse to accept anything but the best, you very often get it!"

On Purpose Goals

Spiritual Qualities
(supports your purpose in this life)

_____

_____

_____

_____

_____

_____

_____

_____

_____

_____

_____

_____

_____

_____

_____

_____

_____

Part II _____

On Purpose Goals

Mental/Emotional Qualities
(temperament, personality, interaction style, attitude toward life)

_____

_____

_____

_____

_____

_____

_____

_____

_____

_____

_____

_____

_____

_____

_____

_____

Part II _____

On Purpose Goals

Physical Qualities
(height, weight, appearance, health/fitness orientation)

_____

_____

_____

_____

_____

_____

_____

_____

_____

_____

_____

_____

_____

_____

_____

_____

Part II _____

Now identify the top six non-negotiable qualities in the entire table and circle them. These top six specific qualities are now identified as **must-haves**. As you meet and interact with potential partners, these serve as mileposts in determining the viability of a future relationship. If you are already in a relationship, this exercise can be used to determine your bottom line requirements and provide you with a powerful discussion tool for clarifying your needs and desires with your partner.

Remember, the non-negotiable goals lay the foundation for your relationships. You are saying, "This is what I want, and I will not settle for less."

After completing your *"Designing Your Own Soul Mate"* list of desired qualities and identified non-negotiables, write the following words in the designated areas at the bottom of each chart, titled Part II: **Who I Am!**

Now, look back over your list and place a star beside every quality you feel you express one hundred percent. Pay attention also to the qualities you don't star. This is not an exercise to put you on a guilt trip. This is an exercise to help you become more aware of your own qualities. It requires a commitment to reality, a commitment to facing yourself as you are without negative judgments.

A key thought here is that people usually like people *who are like themselves*. The adage *"like attracts like"* is true. We tend to become attached to people who mirror how we perceive ourselves from a deep inner level. (There will be more about "reflections" in the **Shared Communications** section of this book.)

Consider reflecting on your **On Purpose Goals** chart to identify personal areas for development. What areas do you need to develop to attract the type of person you desire? An effective and reasonable way to begin is to select one or two items from the qualities you *did not* put a star beside and then focus your attention and efforts to these areas for a month. For example, if one of your goals is to become more compassionate, observe how you respond to other people. Do you listen to what others say? Do you really hear the message both within and behind their words? Can you empathize with them? Can you respond in a loving, caring manner? Take a few items and create a plan of change toward your desired behavior and watch your own personal growth soar. It's your first step toward attracting to yourself the qualities you are now giving others. Now, list your chosen areas on the following page.

Personal Goals Worksheet

AREA FOR DEVELOPMENT

_____

_____

_____

_____

ACTION STEPS

_____

_____

_____

_____

AREA FOR DEVELOPMENT

_____

_____

_____

_____

ACTION STEPS

_____

_____

_____

_____

Personal Goals Worksheet

AREA FOR DEVELOPMENT

_____

_____

_____

_____

ACTION STEPS

_____

_____

_____

_____

AREA FOR DEVELOPMENT

_____

_____

_____

_____

ACTION STEPS

_____

_____

_____

_____

> "First, say to yourself what you would be,
> and then do what you have to do."
> *Epictetus*

Your greatest growth and progress in finding and creating a Soul Mate relationship begins by realizing and *owning* the areas that you need to work on for yourself. It's critical in your journey that you design a plan, outlining personal areas in which you need to grow. But remember: no blame, judgment, or guilt trips are allowed! Blame and judgment are sure-fire prescriptions for suffering. Nor is it acceptable to beat up on yourself. When we try to bring about inner growth or changes through force, we only create a resistance to the natural flow of life energy, which then makes it more difficult to accomplish our goals.

Another little adage worth remembering is *"What you resist, persists!"* Tender, loving care for **yourself** can work wonders. Love yourself into change rather than trying to beat yourself into submission. Become that which you seek.

Turning the Corner

Judith was at a personal crossroads. At age 39, she had been single all her life. And she was ready and more than willing to search for a Soul Mate. After participating in a Soul Mate Workshop, she started attending social functions attended by people with similar interests and goals. She met Kevin, an attractive divorced attorney who a lot of women would consider a real catch. But Judith soon discovered that their interests didn't really mesh. Kevin was interested in someone who would share in travel and social events with no long-term commitment.

In the past, Judith would still have pursued such a relationship, hoping against hope that he would change down the road and be interested in a long-term relationship. This time, though, she was armed with the realization of her primary purpose in life. When Kevin asked her for a date, she told him, frankly but gently, that she was looking for someone who wanted marriage and children and that he seemed to be moving in another direction at this point in his life. Her stomach rumbled and her hands shook, but Judith took pride in having the courage to stand true to her desires, and do so in a caring and loving way.

Judith had turned the corner for good. She was going to wait for a Soul Mate, a man who would be right for her in her journey. For the first time in her life, she understood how important it was to find out upfront whether someone was in alignment with her life goals and non-negotiables. Until the Soul Mate Workshop, she had never really defined them. Now she had a plan, and she would stay focused.

In less than a year, Judith met a man who did align with her goals, a man who was willing to explore a consciously created relationship. A potentially true Soul Mate relationship was in progress! She knew what she wanted. The years of settling for less, and eventually feeling the emotional pain of repeating unhealthy relationships, were over.

"Become that for which you search," counseled St. Francis of Assisi. If you desire a relationship with someone who fits all of the qualities on your *"Designing Your Own Soul Mate"* list, the key to success is to become that for which you search!

"My lover — how shall I describe his face?"

Kabir

Relaxation and Visualization

"You can't depend on your eyes
when your imagination is out of focus!"
Mark Twain

Relaxation is an essential component for guiding your visualizations, the start of your meditative journey to meet your Soul Mate. It offers clarity of focus, easing the "chatter" of the mind.

Relaxation helps us maintain balance in our life, physically, mentally/emotionally, and spiritually. It's also the most effective means of attuning ourselves to the subconscious mind and the spiritual levels within. Relaxation gives us the power to draw toward ourselves the things our hearts desire most: the treasures of life, the gifts that are offered to all of us. It can help us resonate compassionately with the feelings of others. It not only enhances our ability to focus our minds effectively, but also serves as a positive aid for self-awareness.

Visualization is a technique that guides our thought processes in a particular direction, and it's very effective in leading to higher stages of conscious awareness. The next exercise is designed to assist the subconscious mind in magnetizing the "right and ideal" person into your world.

Soul Mate Visualization

"Whatever you can do or dream you can, begin it;
boldness has genius, power, and magic in it."
Johann Wolfgang von Goethe

Find a quiet place where you will not be disturbed, outdoors in a quiet place or inside in your favorite lounging chair. It can be totally quiet or you can play some quiet music, something that soothes the soul. Get comfortable and gently breathe in and out. Mentally and physically, allow your entire being to become at peace. Think these words with conviction, "I give myself permission to fully relax, to be at peace, and to use this time to visualize and meet my ideal Soul Mate, my divine companion."

Close your eyes and visualize yourself stepping forward to begin the journey to meet your Soul Mate. You're in a tranquil wooded area, walking along a quiet path. Your soul is content. You have no fear, only happiness. Birds sing from nearby trees, and a gentle breeze rustles the leaves beneath your feet. Warm sunshine caresses your shoulders. Your cares and concerns have been set aside. You know that today is a gift intended to touch your spirit, to touch your soul.

Take a deep breath and feel it as it goes in and out. Relax your arms, your legs. Ahead on the path, someone is walking toward you. As this person gets closer, you realize it is your ideal Soul Mate. Invite this person to walk with you. Your heart is calm. Your soul tells you this is a friend who cares deeply about you, who wants to share divine contentment with you. With no need to ask for assurance, you know this person is the Soul Mate of your desires. As you meet, you smile at each other and a subtle energy wave flows between you.

At the side of the path, a stone bench sits in the cool shade of a beautiful tree, and its branches reach out as though to welcome you. The two of you move to the bench and sit. No words have been spoken yet; there's no need when two souls have already been joined. An easy conversation then begins. You feel totally safe sharing your dreams and hopes. When your sharing is complete, you both stand up and say farewell. There is joy. You know you will see each other again soon. This is only the beginning, and the best is yet to come. This person wants to know more. This person accepts you as you are. You have never felt so cherished, so loved, so adored. And you offer the same in return: a spiritual acceptance, a completeness and contentment with yourself and with your Soul Mate, a relationship that makes your spirit soar.

You move back to the path, breathing deeply and easily. Every breath affirms the truth of this visualization. The joy of this experience fills your being. Your mind and heart are welcoming this person of your dreams. You now know the meaning of the words "If you can see it, it will be." Life will accomplish the rest!

Memories Yet To Be

Life ... a gift that at times
Seems to lose its rhyme
With its moments moving fast, yet slow ...
Sometimes seems to lose its glow.

But after the thunder of the evening storm
And the morning's sunlight beginning to be born,
Yields a brighter day with a gentle breeze ...
A new beginning, a broken heart freed.

A bird, a flower, a lover's embrace
A day with smiles, a child's face,
A heart that stirs, that longs to see ...
My soul content with memories yet to be.

Robert Krumroy

NOTES:

Overview of Key Concepts and Ideas

- Purpose provides direction, so it is important to stay on track to **who** we are and **what** we desire.
- Identify the **specific qualities** you desire in a Soul Mate, based on how sharing with this person would be an asset to your achieving your purpose in this life. Keep focused and aware of opportunities.
- Three vital elements for achieving your goals are being clear about a desired partner's **spiritual** qualities, **mental/emotional** qualities, and **physical** qualities.
- Remember the mirror concept: "Like attracts like."
- Identify your own personal areas of development and outline a plan for change. **Become that for which you search.**

Four-Step Action Plan

1. Identify and list the spiritual, mental/emotional, and physical qualities you desire in a Soul Mate relationship on the **On Purpose Goals** chart and identify the top six non-negotiables.
2. Review the list of qualities you wrote down and place a star beside every quality you feel you express one hundred percent.
3. Over the coming months, choose one or two items at a time from the list that you wish to develop more fully. Own these qualities and begin to work on changing these areas of yourself for the better.
4. Visualize your Soul Mate at least twice a week. Keep your journey fresh. See your Soul Mate express the qualities that you desire. Feel the acceptance and love that he or she extends to you.

CHAPTER THREE

STAYING AWAKE TO YOUR DREAMS

"Every truth that wakes up in you, changes you."
Angeles Arrien

At this point, you have clearly identified your **purpose** and the specific qualities that are important to you in another person. You have **visualized** your Soul Mate and focused on your own personal qualities you want to develop. You have **committed** to developing within yourself the qualities you desire in others. You are keeping front-of-mind the mirror principle: *Every relationship mirrors an aspect of yourself.*

When you stay aware of your desires and stay on track with who you are and what you desire, relationships fall into place. But beware! It's easy to get off course. Life itself has plenty of distractions that can inadvertently sidetrack you. Realizing your deepest desires doesn't just happen — it requires consciousness, commitment, and courage.

Your next step is to follow a program that will keep you on

track toward the fulfillment of your goals. The best is yet to come, but you must stay focused. *Stay awake to your dreams.* Here's some assistance in accomplishing that.

Retaining Your Personal Power

"Know Thyself."
Inscription at Delphi

Somewhere along the continuum of life we become aware of **power** and **control**. Your mind is your private domain, so you have the right and responsibility to decide how you think and what you believe. But I dare to say that most people have no idea how much power they have to create what they desire.

There is a concept known to Native Americans called *"giving our power away."* You give your power away by thinking negatively and by seeing situations as beyond your control. You also give it away by allowing yourself to become submissive to the wishes or demands of someone else, hoping that it will buy you passage to be "liked" or "included." If you try to live your parent's, best friend's, even your church's expectations, you surrender control of your life and eventually bitterness sets in.

Living someone else's expectations does not bring happiness or keep you on track to your goals. It brings happiness to no one, and it brings you no closer to finding your Soul Mate.

Spiritualist author Jack Kornfield says that the way to be happy is to *"follow your heart and have a strong constitution."* Believe in what you want! See it and claim it. The **ultimate** purpose of relationships is growth into higher levels of self-awareness and expression, the areas of our lives where truth, happiness, and contentment reside. What we receive from a relationship is in direct proportion to what we bring to it. Bringing someone else's expectations contributes nothing to gaining what *you* really want.

Are you giving away your power to others? Are you living who you really are ... or are you living others' expectations?

Are you more negative than positive? Be careful what you say when you talk to yourself. Even if only in your mind, negativity and doubt will steal your dreams.

Create simple strategies for changing these behaviors. Place a rubber band around your wrist as a daily reminder to stay focused on the positive. Tie a small yellow ribbon around something that you see each day to remind you of the same.

Take a moment to reflect. Write down two areas where you may be giving your power away, living someone else's expectations, or being negative about yourself. What can you do to change? Maybe it's just an attitude adjustment. Regardless, it will require a strategy and a "reminder" to change. It will require determination, too. Change doesn't come easy. Bad habits are very hard to break. Remember that what you offer in a relationship is what you will get in return. Lose the negative garbage and wait to see the gifts that return.

AREA TO CHANGE

_____

_____

_____

_____

_____

STRATEGY (Reminder)

_____

_____

_____

_____

_____

IF ACCOMPLISHED, WHAT'S MY PERSONAL GAIN?

_____

_____

_____

_____

_____

AREA TO CHANGE

_____

_____

_____

_____

_____

STRATEGY (Reminder)

_____

_____

_____

_____

_____

IF ACCOMPLISHED, WHAT'S MY PERSONAL GAIN?

_____

_____

_____

_____

_____

Four Rivers of Life

> "The best thing about the future
> is that it comes only one day at a time."
> *Abraham Lincoln*

Another powerful tool you can use in your daily life is the **Four Rivers of Life**. As detailed in Angeles Arrien's book *The Four-Fold Way*, these are four questions — actually four areas of introspection — that indigenous cultures use on a daily basis to stay awake to the wonder of life. The answers you give to those four questions will allow you to track your experiences and personal awareness to the positive experiences life offers.

In starting this exercise, it's a good idea to buy a spiral-bound notebook and label it **Four Rivers of Life**. Each day, enter your answers to the following four questions. This experience will expand your growth, as well as your love for the richness of life.

What *Inspired* You Today?

Everyone has a positive experience to some degree every day.

- What provided a sense of adventure, of wonder, for you?
- What successes did you have today?
- What did you attempt to accomplish that worked out as you had hoped?
- Were there any experiences that brought you out of the **mundane** and lifted you to the **magnificent**?

These are times of joyous exuberance, derring-do, and awesome enthusiasm. Perhaps you had an invincible feeling that you could accomplish whatever you set your heart and mind to accomplish. And did you? What was it?

Recording your successes is not who you hope to be, it's who you are! We rarely give ourselves credit for all the positive things we accomplish. Acknowledge them and celebrate you! As Gandhi affirmed, *"My life is my message."*

What *Challenged* You Today?

What made you grow or stretch out of your comfort zone?

The Navajo people believe that challenges *show us what doors need to be opened and what doors need to be closed.* We often hear the phrase that challenges are simply stepping-stones to greater success — perhaps some of our greatest strengths result from overcoming tough situations. Whenever you are moved (or pushed!) from your comfort zone, life is giving you an opportunity to expand your boundaries. You may kick and scream along the way, but you're certain to find an open door if you're diligent.

There's a saying: *"What we witness, we are changed by."* What challenged you today? What made you grow or stretch, and what was the positive side to the experience or the outcome?

What *Surprised* You Today?

What surprise taught you something important?

A minister friend of mine once asked his congregation: "How would you respond if your dearest friend gave you a bag of rattlesnakes before breakfast?" A curious question coming from a minister, maybe, but a mind-expanding one.

How would you respond? How malleable and flexible are you willing to be? How do you handle the unexpected events that occur daily? Can you see the meaning, the lessons in everything that happens? Can you find humor in even the darkest hour? Can you learn to experience life in a way that exhibits trust for the process of life?

So what surprised you today? And what rich lesson (even if hidden deeply) was learned?

What *Deeply Touched* and *Moved* You Today?

Have you ever stood before a magnificent painting that brought tears to your eyes? Maybe you've watched a breathtaking sunrise or sunset and felt the awe of creation. Or encountered a small child with big, shining eyes who looked up into your face and offered you a seashell. These are things that touch our soul when we are alert to them. They move us in wondrous ways, moments never to be forgotten.

Like wonder, growth, and surprise, the experience of love requires openness or it is lost. Unconditional love requires openness, vulnerability, trust, and faith, an intimacy known only to those who experience it. This love has nothing to do with infatuation or "romantic" love. It's not about contrived sentimentality. It has no focus on "getting;" only on "giving."

Love — deep love, love that accepts, cherishes, and adores you for who you are — is a rare experience. It radiates; it's unmistakably identifiable. It's an experience that so many yearn to find. Have you ever loved "enough" to really let go, to surrender yourself totally and unconditionally? Only then can you realize what a tremendous gift you can receive in exchange!

Pure love is a natural attitude that always reflects good will, kindness, compassion, caring, support, and benevolence. When we live in unconditional love, with a conscious desire to experience and express love, we participate in a most powerful force. And that force radiates from us in all that we experience. It makes us alive and alert to those encounters and experiences that deeply move our souls and touch our inner being.

So what deeply touched and moved you today? Even if you have to search your mind, what event was sent your way to touch your soul, to add meaning and depth to your life?

By taking the time daily to apply the **Four Rivers of Life** to our own lives, we stay awake and alert to the wonder of the daily gifts we receive. We stay attuned to our own dreams and desires, the gifts that are yet to come.

"We do not walk on our legs, but on our will."
Sufi proverb

"Don't Go Back to Sleep"

"The breeze at dawn has secrets to tell you ...
Don't go back to sleep.
You must ask for what you really want ...
Don't go back to sleep.
People are moving back and forth across the
doorsill where the two worlds touch.
The door is round and open ...
Don't go back to sleep."

Rumi

Refusing to walk unconsciously through life lets you experience life on an exhilarating level. But it's all too easy to fall back into old ruts and habits of thinking and doing. A good question to ask yourself every day is "Am I awake or have I gone back to sleep?"

Identify three or more ways you can keep yourself on track. Here are some ideas. You could place the "Don't Go Back to Sleep" poem on your refrigerator door or your bathroom mirror. Or every night for the next month, you could write in your **Four Rivers of Life** journal the answers to the four questions as they applied to that day.

What *Inspired* Me Today?
What *Challenged* Me Today?
What *Surprised* Me Today?
What *Deeply Touched* and *Moved* Me Today?

Share the positive growth experiences and awareness you are making each week with others who support you. Continue to feel the excitement and joy of being alive and the anticipation of the gifts that are yet to come. Thank yourself each day for being willing to do the work to stay awake. Your journey is beginning to progress.

NOTES:

Overview of Key Concepts and Ideas

- Stay awake to your dreams.
- Every relationship mirrors an aspect of yourself.
- The ultimate purpose of a relationship is to grow into higher levels of self-awareness and expression.
- Are you using your personal power to create your experience or are you allowing external issues to induce negativity and doubt?
- The **Four Rivers of Life** are a guide to helping you remain awake, on a daily basis, to the wonderment and growth potential of life. Keep a daily journal and watch your life begin to change. *What inspired you? What challenged you? What surprised you? What deeply touched and moved you?*
- Relaxing and visualizing your ideal relationship helps you stay awake to your dreams. Visualize weekly what you want, the gifts that are yours to form into reality.
- Remember: *"Don't go back to sleep!"* Stay on track to your goals and desires.

Four-Step Action Plan

1. Make a list and review areas where you may have given your power away.
2. Write out your answers to the Four Rivers of Life questions daily, noticing areas that may need greater awareness.
3. Work with the Soul Mate visualization twice a week.
4. Create reminders to help you stay awake.

Shared Reality

CHAPTER FOUR

GATHERING INFORMATION

"He who knows others is wise;
He who knows himself is enlightened."

Lao Tzu

Before beginning your journey of consciously creating and choosing a Soul Mate relationship, it's essential to know in advance the attributes you're seeking. No journey can take you more off course than one that begins with a misguided first step. Until you know *what* you are searching for, stay put. All journeys have enough natural obstacles. Volunteering for a few more due to a lack of a clear destination won't help your quest.

Only when you know *what* you want are you ready to begin observing those persons who might possess the potential for the relationship you desire. Only then is it time to begin determining how compatible another may be for you, to determine whether that someone could potentially be a long-term match.

Important Areas to Explore

Children

Relationship with parents

Co-dependency

Finances (saver or spender)

Extravagant or frugal

Long-term dreams and goals

Childhood experiences

Method for dealing with conflict

Outgoing or homebody

Importance of friends

Spontaneous or structured

Decision maker

Hobbies

Vacation preference

Spiritual preferences

Similar interests

Now, identify areas critical for you to explore with people you meet to quickly determine if they have the necessary qualities that meet your goals.

_____

_____

_____

_____

_____

_____

_____

_____

_____

_____

_____

_____

_____

_____

_____

_____

After identifying specific areas, begin gathering information for deeper understanding and evaluation. Remember, if you don't find out key things before getting involved, your enthusiasm for this relationship is going to have the soaring ability of yesterday's deflated birthday balloons when the negatives come out later. Find out now and avoid deflation later. Don't get blinded by your first encounter. Don't settle. Don't try to fit a round peg into a square hole.

Once you know specifically what you want, finding your Soul Mate is like riding a bus. Don't get discouraged when "Mr. or Ms. Right" doesn't get on at the next stop. With your understanding of your own purpose and feelings, and with your awareness of the Four Rivers of Life, you will recognize them when they appear. Don't settle for less. It's worth the wait!

Gathering Information

"Know how to ask. There is nothing more difficult
for some people, nor for others, easier."
Balthasar Gracian

A powerful way to gather information is by asking questions up front. Most people wait until they have become too attached to another person to ask important questions. Or they don't ask questions for fear of learning that the person is not a match. This is a highly ineffective strategy. Every question either affirms or takes us on a journey closer to where our Soul Mate will be found.

Use the following set of **Power Questions** to get started on the path of discovery. They can help you determine quickly whether the person you're interested in is on track toward where you're going. If you are already in a relationship, the questions will help you clarify what the other person desires for his or her self and for the relationship. Don't worry when answers seem a little uncomfortable. One question and answer doesn't make a conclusion. Rocket scientist Werner von Braun said, *"The only information of any real value to a missile guidance system is when it is not on target."* Our mission is to "get on target."

POWER QUESTIONS:
Getting to the Point Quickly

Power Question Number One:
"HOW SPECIFICALLY?"

The person says to you, "I've spent the last three years really working on myself." That may sound good, but you haven't really learned anything.

Your response is, *"How* specifically did you work on yourself?" If you want to explore their answer even farther, say, "Keep going," or "Tell me more."

Power Question Number Two:
"WHAT SPECIFICALLY?"

The person says to you: "The word *commitment* and I have never gotten along very well." Again, this phrase says very little.

A great question to ask yourself is, "Am I learning everything there is to learn from this statement?" If not, continue by asking, *"What* specifically about commitment hasn't worked well for you?"

Power Question Number Three:
"COMPARED TO WHAT?"

The person says to you, "Your career path seems stagnant." Your response would be, "Stagnant as compared to what?"

Power Question Number Four:
"WHAT WOULD HAPPEN IF ... ?"

Imagine you're in an initial relationship (dating) and the person says, "We have to show up at the dinner party exactly at 7 o'clock."

Your response could be, "What would happen if I have to work late and can't be there at 7 o'clock?"

Asking "What would happen if ... " opens the door for an enlightened discussion and for understanding why another person feels something "has" to be done in a certain way. This approach can help you find out whether this is controlling behavior, rigidity, or if there is a compelling reason for the statement in this situation.

Power Question Number Five:
"ALL, NEVER, EVERYONE?"

This is a good response to sweeping or absolute statements, such as: "We've *never* done it that way before." Or "*Everyone* knows that won't work."

With your most disarming smile, you could ask, "You've never done it that way?" Or you could remark, "Everyone thinks it won't work?" This approach will test the sweeping or absolute nature of the statement. Often you'll find the original assertion was overstated. Your question can spur the other person to a more conscious consideration of the situation and see new realities or possibilities.

In these sample questions, note that I've incorporated a statement that's similar to what the other person said, instead of just asking, "How specifically?" If we go around asking people "How specifically?" or "What specifically?" we may end up sounding like drill sergeants! Incorporating the statement a person has just made will make the **Power Question** more natural and non-confrontational. It also lets people know they have been heard.

For example, a potential partner says, "I have had some pretty challenging relationships in the past." Your response could be: "What specifically about those relationships made them so challenging?" Or you could say in your kindest inquiring way, "Tell me more about that."

To eliminate any friction when asking these questions, pay careful attention to your tone of voice. Ask your questions with loving intentions – in a sincere, interested, and caring manner. You are asking questions solely for clarification. It's important to remember that **ninety percent** of friction is caused by a person's tone of voice. In her book *Are You the One for Me?*, Barbara De Angelis provides hundreds of questions that can help you clarify your areas of interest. Learning to ask questions and then listening carefully to the answers is a skill that will serve you well throughout life.

Use the **Power Questions** to gather more information about a person on all the topics you care deeply about. You'll learn a lot.

For example:

On **Desired Relationships:** "What specifically do you want out of a relationship?"

On **Past Relationships:** "How specifically was your relationship positive or negative?"

On **Past Experiences:** "What specifically about your past relationship do you treasure?"

On **Occupations:** "If you had a chance to do anything you desired, what specifically would you do?"

On **Life's Purpose:** "How specifically would you compare your life at this time to your identified long-term goals and purpose?"

On **Health:** "What specifically about your health would you like to change?"

On **Financial Issues:** "How specifically would you compare your present financial state to your long-term goals?"

These kinds of questions, when appropriately presented, are wonderful conversation starters and can net considerable in-depth information about the other person. You will begin to discover more about them and more about where you want to focus your attention. The strength of any relationship can be measured by the ability to communicate honestly, openly, and sincerely. Asking questions and listening actively are wonderful ways to resolve differences or head off potential conflicts.

Softening the Punch

> "Skill and confidence
> are an unconquered army."
> *George Herbert*

Because **Power Questions** can be extremely direct, you might want to soften their impact by using **Softeners**. These are statements that set the stage for the **Power Question**, and they're relatively easy to get comfortable using. Here are some examples:

"I appreciate what you're saying, *and* ... "
"I think that's a valid point of view, *and* ... "
"I was just wondering ... "
"I'm curious ... "
"I hear what you're saying, *and* ... "

Now, let's put it all together using the **Softener**, the **Power Question**, and the **Restatement**.

Potential partner: "I really learned a lot from my last relationship." Your response: "I hear what you're saying, **and** what specifically did you learn from your last relationship?"

Note in particular my use of the word **and** instead of **but**. As a rule, avoid using **but** in conversations designed to gather information. It's a word that has the uncanny ability to draw lines in the sand and may send the message, "Look out! Some negative information is on its way!"

Also watch out for **why?** in conversations. In our culture, this word tends to elicit a defensive response. Read the following examples and you'll feel the hackles rising a bit even on your neck.

"I appreciate what you're saying, **but** ... "
"I think that's a valid point of view, **but** ... "
"**Why** did you do that?"

By working to clarify the kind of information you're seeking – consciously eliminating those negative buts and whys from your dialog – the quicker you'll arrive at the destination where your Soul Mate is waiting.

Active Listening

"The larger the Island of Knowledge,
the greater the shoreline of wonder."
Ralph Sockman

The other side of asking questions and gathering information is **active listening**. There's an old saying that God gave us two ears and one mouth so we could listen twice as much as we talk. In other words, we would do ourselves a great favor if we focused on hearing more and talking less.

How well you use your ears can play an important part in determining what you learn as you go through life. Have you ever found yourself so busy planning your response that you didn't hear everything that was being said? It's a common mistake. Listening takes energy. It's a skill that few people perfect.

One of the major reasons so many relationships break down is that the parties involved have not learned to listen. Listening is a learned skill. When we develop it to the fullest, we increase our capacity to learn and we enhance our ability to maintain healthy relationships.

Active listening necessitates staying focused on what the speaker is saying. The more we listen and learn, the better the person we become, and the better our evaluation skills become for determining whether a potential relationship is worth pursuing.

NOTES:

Overview of Key Concepts and Ideas

- The more we know about others (preferably up front), the wiser we can be in determining potential long-term compatibility.
- Asking appropriate questions is an excellent way of gathering information.
- **Listening** is as important as **asking!**

Five-Step Action Plan

1. Identify specific areas of interest for determining whether a person is on track for your purpose and goals.
2. Review the **Power Questions** and commit them to memory so they're available for easy use at any time.
3. Ask your questions in a sincere, interested, and caring manner. Use "and" instead of "but." Be careful about using "why?"
4. Develop the skill of active listening.
5. Begin using information-gathering questions to discover possibilities.

Part I

SHARED REALITY

CONCLUSION

You have now learned the first foundational principle for creating or drawing a Soul Mate relationship into your life. As Neale Donald Walsch explains in his book and audiotape series *Friendship with God,* there are three tools of creation: **Thoughts, Words,** and **Deeds.** By focusing your thoughts, words, and actions in a concise, awake, and aware way, you begin the process of creating your highest desires.

SUMMARY
The Components of Shared Reality

- Identifying your purpose and desired feelings.
- Defining your *"ideal Soul Mate relationship"* by writing down what you want and noting your six non-negotiables.
- Imagining every day that your perfect Soul Mate or companion exists within your life.

- Becoming that for which you search by creating a personal self-development plan with action steps.
- Staying awake to your dreams. Don't allow them to become blurred and compromised. *"Don't go back to sleep!"*
- Identifying areas of importance to know about others.
- Gathering information by asking questions to discover whether a potential relationship may exist.
- Deepening your understanding through active listening.

As you work through the Soul Mate processes, you will find truths about yourself and others that can bring dramatic change and happiness to your life and to those around you. Stay in alignment with the spiritual side of yourself and let your joy in life shine. Declare, experience, express, and fulfill who you really are!

SHARED COMMUNICATIONS

The Second Foundational Key

"We are not influenced by everything we read or learn.
In one sense, and perhaps the deepest, we ourselves
determine the influences we are submitting to."

Alexandre Koyre

CHAPTER FIVE

THE CREATION OF BELIEFS

"Discovery follows discovery;
each both raising and answering questions;
each ending a long search and each
providing the new instruments for a new search."
J. Robert Oppenheimer

"How Did I Get Here?"

Anna was a go-getter, that was for sure. Determined to make good in her first job out of college, she happily worked late at the office a couple of nights a week. And soon it became her everyday routine. Her superiors loved her enthusiasm for exceeding their expectations, and their accolades inspired Anna to work even longer hours. To them, she was a superwoman.

Even after her marriage to David, Anna kept up her 70-hour

workweek. In her "spare" time, she was running her home, attending night school, visiting a senior citizens retirement center, and going to church three times a week! Need something done? Ask Anna. She never says no.

But what of her relationship with David? Just eight months after their wedding, Anna was pulling away from him emotionally. She always had other things to do. *David would just have to understand. And he would, certainly he would!* Without realizing it, Anna was beginning to create the same type of relationship she had witnessed between her parents. She was playing out the same behavior she swore she would never do, and she was becoming an angry person.

David wasn't perfect, but she knew that when they were dating. Still, she liked him and felt that "becoming a couple" would require only slight adaptations on both of their parts. Anna thought she had learned how to speak up when David crossed boundaries. She thought she knew how to effectively express how she needed his support. Instead, she was finding it all too easy to get frustrated, and eventually she began to withdraw. "Why bother?" she told herself. "It's no big deal."

Of course, it turned out to be a very big deal. Anna's desperation eventually made her feel she was doomed to repeat the life of loneliness she had seen in her parents. Her despair was chilling. Marriage was supposed to be filled with excitement and shared dreams. Hers had quickly turned into a shared journey of loss.

Anna was wracked with agonizing questions. How did she get here? How did she re-create the very thing she didn't want? Why was she driven to repeat behaviors that were inexorably leading to divorce?

Many of us can identify with Anna's cry of "How did I get *here?*" It's a question you might pose after repeated squabbles with a lover, or when a squabble feels more like an explosion and the repercussions last for days. Maybe you had a power struggle at work, and it seemed awfully similar to other confrontations you had encountered. Whatever the situation, if you can identify a pattern, it may be worth a further look.

Shared Communications is about taking a close look at relationship patterns and beginning to understand how these patterns play a role in our having or not having what we truly desire. Shared Communications between Soul Mates is a mutual understanding of how their past has made them who they are today. It means being willing to own and accept your own strengths as well as your shortcomings. It means consciously working with each other to help heal the wounds from your past.

> "Beliefs drive our intentions,
> which create thoughts,
> which lead to deeds,
> which become habits,
> that harden into character,
> which shapes our world."
> *Jack Kornfield*

Our challenge is to identify beliefs that do not serve us well in relationships and to begin a personal journey of healing and transformation. Let's look at how beliefs are created.

Life on Two Levels: *Conscious and Unconscious*

"One gets larger impressions in boyhood, sometimes,
which he has to fight against all his life."

Mark Twain

The **conscious mind** is the foundation of perception: how you react to everything you see, hear, and feel. The conscious mind allows us to see the beauty of the earth, sea, and sky; hear the lovely strains of music; feel a whole range of emotions. Each of us can have different interpretations, reactions, and emotional responses to the same event.

The **unconscious mind**, sometimes called the subconscious mind, is our memory mind. It's the home of our habits: the interpretation of our past thoughts and experiences. The work of overcoming or changing relationship habits and beliefs takes place primarily in this part of our mind. The unconscious mind is the source of most of the obstacles we stumble over in our relationships.

The Baby Factor

We all come into this life with open minds and open hearts. Then this young, open human being begins to program its mind so it can survive and function in the world. Like a computer, that tiny mind begins absorbing all the data it can from family members, friends, and everybody else who moves into its sphere. And from that activity comes the dawning of beliefs and ideals about how the world should be — *and they will change very little, without intervention, over a lifetime!*

That statement may sound fantastic, but it's true. Most of your personality is completely formed by the time you're six years old. And new research is beginning to point to an even earlier age. Though lacking the emotional maturity to understand how life works on a big scale, these little people are nevertheless making up their minds about how life is and should be. This information makes up the content of our subconscious minds.

Creating Beliefs about Ourselves

"Let us not look back in anger or forward in fear,
but around in awareness."
James Thurber

What we hear, see, and feel as young children make deep and lasting impressions. In fact, these early experiences largely create our beliefs about our self-worth and what we deserve in life. And as our subconscious mind develops, we begin to live by those beliefs and carry them forward into our adult life.

Unfortunate as it is, a young child's subconscious can draw profoundly misguided conclusions from both positive and negative experiences – and those conclusions become the package of reality we carry throughout life. Regardless of the infinitely greater emotional and intellectual capabilities we develop later, our lives are still tied closely to those earliest perceptions about our self-worth, our abilities, and our needs – *beliefs that are often counter-productive and totally unrealistic.* Even so, they repeatedly drive us into situations that match the expectations in our subconscious minds.

The final result is that we build emotional walls to protect ourselves from experiences we found painful as young children. Until we consciously recognize and resolve our unhealed wounds from the past, our life's journey continues to go around in a circle. And we're left to wonder time and again why we always return to the pain we so desperately want to avoid.

Through the Eyes of a Child

When I was five years old, my dad left the family and didn't return for 23 years. He had been a cold and distant father, but I believed he loved me even though he couldn't show it. I wanted him to hold me and tell me how much he loved me, but that didn't happen and then he was gone.

So at the tender age of five, all I knew was that my father loved me and that he had abandoned me. I couldn't comprehend the many other factors that had nothing to do with me, one being that he was an alcoholic. As a result, the only sense I could make of the situation was that he left because of me. If I had been a better little girl, my mind told me, Dad would still be here. And I believed that devoutly, despite my mom's consistent reinforcement that I was not to blame in any way and that his leaving had nothing to do with me.

As the years passed, the conclusions I had drawn from those traumatic times became part of the deep programming of my unconscious mind. I kept telling myself I had "worked through the pain" and survived as a "whole person." Like Anna, I became a workaholic, unconsciously trying to prove I was a good person. It wasn't until my mid-30s that I saw the reality of that childhood damage in the relationships I was choosing. I was unconsciously attracted to men like my father!

When I met nice, kind, and emotionally sensitive men, I labeled them as "too nice" or "too boring." My subconscious had modeled its definition of a "desirable" man on my first love — Dad — and that meant seeking out people who were difficult and distant. My programming was telling me that relationships had to be difficult. I thought that overcoming difficulty and pain was the highest level of love!

On a conscious level, I really did want a good, nice, kind man. But my emotional, subconscious mind steered me the other way and I fell into a pattern of painful and frustrating relationships without knowing what was happening to me.

I finally understood everything when I learned how the subconscious mind works. This knowledge cleared up a lot of confusion. At the same time, it didn't make me blame my mom and dad. I truly believe that most parents do the best they can with the sincerest of intentions.

Change is the Thing

So, how do we become aware of our belief systems and change them? How do we stop repeating the pain? First, you must learn the importance of this statement: *"What you have in your life is what you are willing to be in your life."*

If a particular situation has a way of repeating itself in your life, in some way and on some level you have a belief system that says, "This is what I deserve" or "This is how things should be." Relationships are a window to the conscious beliefs we want to reinforce and the subconscious beliefs we need to change. As painful and uncomfortable issues arise, life is saying, *"Hey, pay attention! You have work to do here!"* We continue drawing the same kind of experiences to ourselves until we have finally had enough and answer the wake-up call.

Getting Our Belief System History Straight

"What a gift of grace to be able to take the chaos from within and from it create some semblance of order."

Katherine Paterson

To free yourself from painful relationship patterns, you must first break through barriers buried deep within your subconscious mind — namely, those unhealthy belief systems you've been saddled with since childhood. The starting point is to bring your unconscious intentions to conscious awareness and then to remember: *Every relationship you have in your life is perfectly designed to give you exactly what you have based — on your belief systems!*

A powerful exercise called **History Gathering** will help you unlock those old, hidden beliefs that are possibly keeping you from experiencing the joy and happiness you deserve in life.

I want to emphasize that this exercise is not about dumping on your parents; it's about uncovering your past and then choosing to adopt healthier beliefs. Therapist Harville Hendricks, Ph.D., is the creator of this exercise. He published it in his book *Getting the Love You Want,* and he uses it extensively with great success in his workshops. It helped me. Let's see if it helps you in your own journey of self-discovery.

The History Gathering Exercise

"It's a sad day when you find out that it's not an accident or time or fortune but yourself that kept things from you."

Nancy Thayer

Prepare for this exercise by getting very comfortable. Take long, slow breaths. This gives your body the signal to relax. Focus your conscious mind on your breathing and begin to think about events from your early childhood. Try to think deeply about the impressions and influences that might have shaped your belief systems years and years ago.

Begin the exercise by answering the following questions. Don't spend too much time on each question, but be as specific, detailed, and in depth as possible.

A. List three or four *negative* characteristics of the primary caretaker(s) who raised you during your first six years of life. (Parents, grandparents, guardians, etc.)

_____

_____

_____

_____

_____

_____

B. List three or four *positive* characteristics of the primary caretaker(s) who raised you during your first six years of life. (Parents, grandparents, guardians, etc.)

_____

_____

_____

_____

_____

_____

C. List what you wanted and needed as a child from your caretaker(s) that you didn't receive enough of. For example: *Listen to me. Hold me. Tell me I was a good girl/boy. Tell me I was wonderful.*

_____

_____

_____

_____

_____

_____

D. List the positive feelings you experienced as a child. (Write feelings only.) For example: *Felt proud of myself. Felt strong, smart, happy, excited.*

_____

_____

_____

_____

_____

_____

E. What did you actually do when you were scared, hurt, or frustrated? Reflect on two or three of the most difficult times. For example: *Did you withdraw, go numb inside, act out?*

_____

_____

_____

_____

_____

_____

After completing the **History Gathering Exercise**, take your answers and place them on the corresponding lines (A, B, C, etc.) of the **Unconscious Agenda Exercise.**

The Unconscious Agenda Exercise

"Loyalty to petrified opinion never yet broke a chain
or freed a human soul."

Mark Twain

I tend to be drawn to people who are *(a)* _____

_____

_____,

In order to get them to *(b)* _____

_____

_____,

So that I can get *(c)* _____

_____

_____,

And feel *(d)* _____

_____

_____,

I sometimes stop myself from getting what I want by *(e)* _____

_____

_____.

This exercise will help you identify what some of your belief systems about relationships may be. It can also provide insights about why you're drawn to the same kind of person and experiences, and why you end up with the same results time after time.

Now take a moment and list below where the items identified in the Unconscious Agenda exercise have shown up in your life in some way. Another question to ask yourself is how past or present relationships mirror in some way the behaviors — *negative and positive* — of your primary caretakers.

Connecting the Past and Present

_____

_____

_____

_____

_____

We humans go through life unconsciously seeking someone who will help us heal our wounds from the past. When we feel a strong attraction for someone, it's a signal from our subconscious that here is a person with a similar past — a person who might help us re-create and bring closure to our childhood experiences. Here is a person, our subconscious says, who can help us work through and heal the pain and help us grow into *wholeness*.

Partners who are already aware of their own past are a gift! They understand what you're going through and can give you the space you need as you begin to change your belief systems and create healthier, happier relationship strategies. Most people, however, keep choosing partners who unconsciously join in a painful replay of experiences from the past. And the cycle of rejection, pain, loneliness, and unhappiness begins again.

Mother Love Gone Awry

Tom's mother was the dominant influence in his young life. She held the reins of the household and brooked no interference, no other points of view. His dad's role in the house was helper. Mom handled — controlled — everything and everybody.

Her need to control became even more pronounced after she suffered a stroke when Tom was eleven. Her lingering disability left her even more opinionated and angry at life, and she kept herself emotionally distant from Tom. He was twenty-one years old before he ever heard her say, "I love you." And that was on her deathbed.

His mother's death, far from giving Tom a sense of closure to a difficult childhood, unconsciously launched him on a quest that would result in a life of struggle for the next twenty years. That's because he chose to marry the only girl Mom had ever approved of.

Tom and Brenda had met in college. She was a cheerleader; he was on the football team. Everyone remarked what a great-looking couple they made. But it was his mother's opinion that meant the most to Tom. She told him Brenda would be good for him; she would keep him on the straight and narrow. He had finally met her approval. And even though she was gone now, he would honor that. A short time after his mother's death, Tom and Brenda were married.

Many times when people marry young, their partner is practically a reincarnation of the parent they had the greatest emotional struggle with as a child. This was the case with Brenda. She was rigid and judgmental. Everything was black and white; most people were wrong. Before Tom finally walked out twenty long, unhappy years later, they had struggled through six psychologists trying to salvage the marriage.

There's a tendency to blame a divorce on the partner who leaves, but it isn't that simple. Divorces usually result from issues that both parties act out, entirely unconsciously. Fixing blame in a divorce is like fixing blame for the wrinkles in the bed in the morning. Wrinkles, like the factors behind a breakup, are made totally unconsciously. Both parties make them. Both parties are one hundred percent responsible.

Tom's story, which he related during a Soul Mate Workshop, didn't have a fairytale "happy ending." But it did have a healthy one. After the divorce, he and Brenda sought each other's forgiveness and became friends. They both realized they had needed a wake-up call, that staying together would have just continued the pain and the cycle of despair. They now know that life offers so much more, and they have the opportunity to grow into healthier, happier people.

An Issue of Trust

Nancy's strongest childhood memories were of evenings spent at nightclubs and country clubs. Her mother played the piano in a dance band and dragged the little girl along when she entertained. Nancy's father was seldom around, and when he was she remembers him as an authoritarian. Neither parent was "emotionally or legally available," as she put it.

It's not surprising that Nancy grew up unable to trust and that she leaned on authority figures. For years, an abandonment issue would keep her from giving the love she so desperately wanted in return. Happily, she told fellow workshop participants, that was changing now. The catalyst was a new partner who had encouraged her to "pick up the shovel and dig deep into your early life." When she did, Nancy recognized the broken record of her unhappy past experiences.

At the time she attended the workshop, Nancy was working to clear up unfinished business with her parents, and this was bringing about a healing in her relationship with them. She had also begun to put herself in healthy situations where she could practice trust. She was beginning to recognize how she was consciously and unconsciously choosing unhealthy relationships. She was most definitely on the journey to *wholeness*.

NOTES:

Overview of Key Concepts and Ideas

- We approach life on two levels: conscious and unconscious.
- Our experiences with our caretakers before the age of six — and most likely even earlier — contribute to the creation of our strongest relationship beliefs.
- Our beliefs deeply influence what we create for ourselves in relationships.
- It is important to bring our unconscious intentions to conscious awareness.
- What keeps showing up in our life is a mirror about what we believe about relationships.

Two-Step Action Plan

1. Complete the **History Gathering** and **Unconscious Agenda** exercises.
2. Note where you see these same patterns showing up in your life, as identified in the exercises.

CHAPTER SIX

CHANGING BELIEFS

"Each relationship you have with another person
reflects the relationship you have with yourself."

Alice DeVille

Everyone has the capacity to live a life of abundance and fulfillment. First, however, you need to reprogram the false belief
patterns that interfere with your life's journey. You begin this
process by accepting that, as an adult:

- You create your experience of life.
- You are only a victim if you choose to be.

The next step is believing that what you have in your life is
what you *allow to be in your life*. Think about this statement for
a moment. If a particular situation in your life continually repeats

itself, you have a belief system that says, "This is what I deserve" or "This is what life is, this is what reality is." It's only when you choose to surrender your past that you allow yourself to be fully alive in the present. Only then will you be able to accept the wonderful gifts that the universe offers each of us.

Managing Your Mind ... So It Doesn't Manage You!

> "It's when we're given choices
> that we sit with the gods and design ourselves!"
> *Dorothy Gilman*

You can't change the past, but you can manage your mind so the past doesn't manage you. By becoming conscious of your belief patterns, you can learn to make appropriate choices and take charge of your life.

You can decide to stop unwittingly sabotaging your relationships and your lives. Each of us is responsible for creating the conditions, beliefs, and thoughts that draw people, experiences, and events into our lives.

There are three steps to getting what you truly want:

- **The thoughts you think**
- **The words you speak**
- **The actions you take**

Positive thinking is absolutely essential for promoting positive feelings, behaviors, and results. Positive thinking has been described as looking at whatever is true and seeing the situation as positive and desirable. Only then can you make the choice to live your life deliberately, harmoniously, and creatively. Only then can you live in awareness of the moment instead of in a reflection of your past. Life is more than a process of discovery. It is a process of **creating**.

Six Strategies for Recognizing Outdated Beliefs

"I left the woods for as good a reason I went there.
Perhaps it seemed to me that I had several more lives to live
and could not spare any more time for that one."
Henry David Thoreau

Here are six powerful strategies for recognizing outdated beliefs and making the changes needed to begin experiencing the relationship you desire.

1. BE AWARE.

Choose to become consciously aware of the things that keep showing up and bringing you unhappiness. Choose to **own** the belief system that drives you toward these choices. This is how you begin to move in a more positive, happy, and fulfilling direction.

Do you see yourself in any of these unhealthy belief systems?

- Consistently choosing partners who won't commit to a long-term relationship.
- Finding partners who are not emotionally available.
- Finding partners who reinforce a belief system that you're not good enough.

On the following page, make a list of your positive relationship patterns and a list of your negative relationship patterns.

All patterns listed in the Negative column are life's way of saying, *"Pay attention! Something in this area is not in alignment with where you say you want to go!"* Every time you repeat a negative pattern, you make it stronger. Awareness is the first step to changing a pattern.

Establishing a concrete plan for change is the next step. Example: If you're interested in a long-term relationship, but you repeatedly choose partners who are not, set guidelines for asking questions upfront. As soon as you learn they're not interested in a long-term relationship, you agree to move on immediately.

It's worth noting that the world around us doesn't always encourage us to be healthy! Songs with lyrics like *"I can't live without you," "my heart is breaking,"* and *"I'll never love again"* can actually have quite an effect on reinforcing your negative belief systems, especially if you repeat the words to yourself. The negativity you see on television is even less subtle. Now, I'm not suggesting that you tune out TV, radio, movies, the Internet, or whatever, but you should remain aware of how outside influences affect you and the changes you desire. There's an old computer term, "Garbage in, garbage out." What you put into your mental computer forms the results that come out.

2. CANCEL/CANCEL! RESET!

You have the power to stop negative thoughts from penetrating your mind. When you hear someone, or even yourself, say something that is definitely not what you wish to claim, use the

RELATIONSHIP PATTERNS

POSITIVE

_____

_____

_____

_____

_____

_____

_____

_____

_____

_____

NEGATIVE

_____

_____

_____

_____

_____

_____

_____

_____

_____

_____

_____

"Cancel/Cancel" or "Reset" technique to zap it. It may sound ridiculous at first, but saying those words out loud actually sends a signal to the brain that you forbid the entry of negative thoughts. By abruptly halting a thought or pattern, you begin to reverse its impact on your life. My friends and I have an agreement to say "Cancel/Cancel!" whenever we hear each other saying negative things. It keeps you focused on what you want ... and it's also fun.

3. USE A LANGUAGE OF CHOICE.

The words you speak have a tremendous impact on the quality of your life. So be careful what you say when you talk to yourself. Telling yourself how stupid, worthless, or undeserving you are can bring more of the same. It reinforces a false belief and continues the journey that has already caused you so much pain. Our language affects our thinking and feeling because the mind believes what it hears — especially when the words come out of your own mouth!

Some words limit your choices and negatively affect your feelings. When you hear yourself say, "I can't," consider the difference it makes to say instead, "I will not." Or instead of "It's my fault," say "It's my responsibility." And finally, ask yourself, "What can I learn from this?" instead of proclaiming, "What a mess!" You will see a remarkable change in yourself.

4. REVIEW PAST SUCCESSES.

"The most important skill is to learn from individual experiences, our own and others," says psychoanalyst Edward

Shapiro. You gain much wisdom by reflecting on past relationships and identifying the positive things you've learned. The positive things you recall remind you of growth experiences that have enriched your life.

Never apologize for your past experiences — they helped you become the person you are today. It's been said that "experience is the toughest teacher because she gives the test first and then the lesson," but many of the lessons are actually blessings. Your own pain may have caused you to become more sensitive to other people's pain. A financial setback may have caused you to learn compassion for others or to appreciate the simple gifts of life.

And that leads us to your next exercise. In this one, I want you to identify five people who taught you valuable and positive lessons or assisted you in becoming the person you are today. These people may represent challenging relationships or supportive ones. This is a powerful exercise in honoring your past and acknowledging the stepping-stones of our lives. And it also frees you to move forward.

Name

_____

Provided these positive lessons and awareness for my growth.

_____

_____

_____

Name

_____

Provided these positive lessons and awareness for my growth.

_____

_____

_____

Name

_____

Provided these positive lessons and awareness for my growth.

_____

_____

_____

Name

_____

Provided these positive lessons and awareness for my growth.

_____

_____

_____

Name

_____

Provided these positive lessons and awareness for my growth.

_____

_____

_____

5. REMEMBER, NEGATIVE THINKING IS ONLY TEN PERCENT ACCURATE.

Ninety percent of what you fear will never happen and thank goodness for that! When you worry and obsess — *"awfulize"* — you're doing nothing but stealing from today's happiness.

6. PRACTICE AFFIRMATIONS.

Affirmations are positive statements that something is already so. It's sort of like "fake it until you make it." When you consistently repeat negative statements to yourself, you reinforce those beliefs in your unconscious. On the following page are some of the most common negative statements I hear about relationships. Next to each one is an example of how to change those statements to a positive perspective.

Affirmations

Dealing with Internal Relationship Busters

Negative:	Positive:
Relationships are a hassle and are more trouble than they're worth.	Conscious, aware relationships are fun and enjoyable. They work out for my highest good.
My relationships never work out.	My commitment and courage create relationships that are deeper and more meaningful.
I'm not creative. I can't think that way.	I am open to creativity. Wherever I am, I am in the right place, engaged in the right activity to get ideas.
Every time I talk to him/her, we argue.	Every time I talk to him/her, we create an opportunity for greater understanding.
There are no potential Soul Mates in this town.	I meet potential Soul Mates regularly who live in my town.
I just don't know ...	I feel comfortable making any decision.

Now, identify and write down what you feel is your most common internal negative message about relationships.

_____

_____

_____

_____

_____

_____

_____

Now do a flip-flop. Create a powerful affirmation for yourself. Hint: It's sometimes helpful to start with "I am now ... " If you begin acting as if this affirmation is already happening, you will believe it. And it will be.

I am now *(finish the sentence)* ...

_____

_____

_____

_____

_____

_____

_____

Soul Mate Affirmation

"Man is made by his belief.
As he believes, so he is."

Bhagavad-Gita

I attended a workshop several years ago in which the instructor shared an affirmation created by the Indian spiritual master Paramahansa Yogananda. The affirmation was designed to assist in "manifesting" a Soul Mate.

Yogananda said that if you repeated this affirmation twice a day for six months and did the necessary internal healing to let a Soul Mate into your life, the ideal Soul Mate would appear. This affirmation isn't magic; its purpose is to help you begin building your faith that a Soul Mate relationship is possible. The point is: When "you know that you know" a certain type of relationship is possible, you have laid the foundation for creating this or anything else in your life.

Yogananda said the affirmation also works for people who are already in a relationship. For these people, stating the affirmation can bring to the surface areas not in alignment with their dreams and goals. Whatever the outcome, it can open new doors to greater happiness.

Affirmations are powerful stuff, because when we begin to announce to life who we are and what we believe, everything that is not in alignment with our declaration shows up. Our conscious declaration of who we are and what we want then serves as a road map that aligns our highest desires with our conscious goals. The outcome is nothing short of the best of what life wants us to have.

The Affirmation

*_____, *Bless me*
that I choose my life's companion
according to the law of perfect soul union.

* Feel free to start the affirmation with whatever name honors your specific spiritual beliefs.

I began using this affirmation by saying it many times a day. (I'm still working on avoiding excess!) I had notes on the bathroom mirror, the car dashboard, in my desk drawer at work. And who's to say that excess doesn't work? Within six months, I had met my Soul Mate and I'm still smiling! Six wonderful years later, I still know that life gave me a gift that I only had to be willing to claim and receive.

The One and Only – or One of Many?

This is a good time to make a point about the nature of Soul Mates. Many people believe there is only one Soul Mate per person, per life. That has not been my experience, and I don't believe it's true for anybody. As we grow in our own awareness, we learn there may be many potential Soul Mates who would be wonderful companions. Healing our wounds from the past opens our eyes and attracts others to us. There is no reason why it would happen only once.

Many people also believe they've blown their chances forever if a Soul Mate relationship – or what they think could have been a Soul Mate relationship – doesn't work out. Again, not true, for the same reasons as above. So relax and let go of this fraudulent belief system. People who chronically mope about "the one that got away" are missing the joy that life has to offer. You can't change the past. Focus on the present. What we have and what we can focus on is this moment — *now* — and the opportunity to live it fully.

Evicting the "Yeah, but" Family

"It's never too late — in fiction or in life — to revise."

Nancy Thayer

Each of us has thoughts embedded in our subconscious that have unbelievable power to inflict fear and remind us of all our self-induced limits. They're members of what we call the "Yeah, but" Family, insidious triggers that invite negative self-talk into our consciousness. It's especially true when something has "heart" meaning. If you're not aware of your resident triggers, you can be unwittingly sabotaging your stated desires, such as creating a Soul Mate relationship.

Here's an exercise that will help you identify these enemies and root them out. On the top of the worksheet on the following page, list all the reasons you tell yourself you can have a Soul Mate relationship. Take as much time as you need. It's important to really identify the supportive thoughts. Then, list on the bottom all the reasons you tell yourself you cannot have this relationship.

Why I CAN Have This

_____

_____

_____

_____

_____

_____

_____

_____

_____

_____

_____

Why I CAN'T Have This

_____

_____

_____

_____

_____

_____

_____

_____

_____

_____

Now, cross out every entry you made on the bottom of the worksheet on page 129 and restate each of them as an affirmation below. Begin each with:

"I am now ...

1. _____

2. _____

3. _____

4. _____

5. _____

6. _____

Substituting affirmations for self-imposed negative statements helps you reprogram your mind to a new positive direction and supports your goal to enjoy the best that life has to offer. Don't delay. It's time to send the "Yeah, But" family packing!

NOTES:

Overview of Key Concepts and Ideas

- Manage your mind so it doesn't manage you.
- There are six strategies for changing outdated beliefs.
- Affirmations provide a way of redirecting our attention.
- The Soul Mate affirmation helps us build our belief that a Soul Mate relationship is possible.
- There are many potential Soul Mates for each of us. Clinging to the belief that only one exists for us in the entire universe blinds us to opportunities.
- By recognizing the "Yeah, but" Family of thoughts, we can begin the process of reinforcing what we truly desire.

Seven-Step Action Plan

1. Notice patterns and events that keep showing up in your life.
2. Identify beliefs that may be driving the patterns you would like to change and begin a plan to heal them.
3. Notice your negative thoughts and change them to positive affirmations.
4. Identify five people from your past and how they were stepping-stones to your growth.
5. State your Soul Mate affirmation at least twice a day to affirm your belief.
6. Identify the most common negative messages you have about relationships and create a positive affirmation to change them.
7. Identify the **"Yeah, but"** thoughts in your subconscious that trigger and reinforce negativity about yourself. Replace each one with an affirmation.

CHAPTER SEVEN

RELATIONSHIP PATTERNS

"Reflection is the opposite of blame."
C. Otto Scharmer

As you become more aware of your thoughts, words, and deeds, and the impact they have on your daily life, an area of additional awareness that can support your growth is understanding **Denial, Indulgence,** and **Integrity,** the three relationship patterns identified by Angeles Arrien. If not managed properly, two of these patterns can create havoc in your life.

Denial patterns include such behaviors as avoidance, covering up, and evasion. **Indulgence** patterns cause us to obsess, wallow, worry, play out being a victim, and exaggerate our conclusions.

The Denial and Indulgence patterns are based on fear, and whenever fear is present in a relationship, love cannot exist. They signal the presence of fear, and fear keeps us from healing and experiencing joy. Nearly all relationships that include unhealthy interactions typically are hexed by Denial or Indulgence, or both. The **Integrity** pattern, on the other hand, is one to celebrate! It brings exhilarating fulfillment and happiness, and it's typically present in Soul Mate relationships. This pattern is based on genuine and complete love. There is trust, openness, and vulnerability.

Relationship Patterns

Denial	Indulgence	Integrity
Behaviors	*Behaviors*	*Behaviors*
1. Avoidance	1. Obsessiveness	1. Authenticity
2. Chooses not to address	2. Wallowing	2. Trust
3. Covers up	3. Worrying	3. Openness
4. Evades conflict	4. Victimhood	4. Truth
5. Withholds	5. Exaggerating	5. Vulnerability

Used with permission of Angeles Arrien, Ph.D., *The Four-Fold Way.*

Changing Unhealthy Relationship Patterns

In this exercise, list behaviors you exhibit in relationships (past or present) that fall under Denial or Indulgence patterns. Write the impact they have had on your relationships.

Behavior

_____

Impact

_____

_____

_____

Behavior

_____

Impact

_____

_____

_____

Behavior

_____

Impact

_____

_____

_____

Behavior

_____

Impact

_____

_____

_____

Behavior

_____

Impact

_____

_____

_____

Now identify what commitments you are willing to make to change these unhealthy patterns to healthy ones. Example: "Instead of evading conflict with Joanne, I will practice speaking up. I will also take a class on conflict so I can do it in a healthy and respectful way."

_____

_____

_____

_____

_____

_____

Three Universal Fears

"It is not that you must be free from fear.
The moment you try to free yourself from fear,
you create a resistance against fear.
Resistance, in any form, does not end fear.
What is needed, rather than
running away or controlling or suppressing
or any other resistance, is understanding fear;
that means, watch it, learn about it,
come directly into contact with it.
We are to learn about fear,
not how to escape from it, not how to resist it
through courage and so on."

J. Krishnamurti

Earlier in this book, we talked about the role that fear plays in our lives if we let it. To heal your wounds and create a positive relationship, you need to learn how to make fear your ally instead of your enemy.

Understanding the two basic emotions that drive us as human beings — Love and Fear — is our beginning point. These emotions impact virtually everything you experience in life. Love drives happiness and joyfulness. Fear is behind sadness, anger, and depression.

Dr. Jim Farr, a noted psychologist in the field of self-awareness, used to astound and energize clients by telling them they needed to be afraid only one or two percent of the time. *And that was when they were in actual physical danger!*

Most of us are totally unaware that fear runs our lives as much as 97 percent of the time. And there's a real danger in letting that happen. Fear can destroy your health, drain you of energy, and cause you to overreact in many situations.

Our fears aren't even grounded in the here and now. Most fear is **of the future.** We let our minds jump ahead to "what might happen," and our fears grow to dreadful proportions. *Even though virtually none of these awful scenarios ever come to pass.*

I have to confess to first-hand knowledge.

About four years ago, I attended a workshop on self-development in Arizona. Three days and nights of the twelve-day program consisted of going into the desert alone with a tent, hemp rope, sleeping bag, and water. The Native Americans do this as a spiritual journey for cleansing their spirits and minds and receiving clarity on their purpose. Such was our quest as well.

The hemp rope's role was supposedly to keep snakes out of our tent area. *Snakes?* About half an hour after setting up my tent, I started looking at the rope that surrounded it. I have a pretty good imagination, and it locked onto what a snake would look like if it suddenly appeared. Would its eyes be huge or small? How long would it be? How aggressive would it be? Would it bite me?

You'll note that all my thoughts were in the future!

Within fifteen minutes, I was terrorized. And we had just arrived — there were still three days and nights to go. Then my mind upped the stakes. What if this snake does bite me? Would I die? Without even realizing it, I was reinforcing a pattern of fear within my mind.

Well, no snake ever showed up. All that happened was that I had invented a negative pattern that stole joy from my day and delayed the fulfillment of my goals.

The Awful Facts about Fear

We now know quite a lot about the origin of fear. It's usually based on three factors: (1) Not feeling worthy; (2) Fear of trusting others and "awfulizing" our assumptions; or (3) Abandonment/ separation. Let's look at these three Universal Fears individually for a clearer picture. These descriptions are from Gregg Braden's *Walking between the Worlds*.

1. ABANDONMENT/SEPARATION

Definition:

Relationships in which we are devastated when they fail or fall apart.

Unwanted Consequence:

You may feel like you are always the one who gets "left" in the relationship. You may find yourself leaving a good relationship as a form of protection so you don't get hurt if the other person leaves first.

2. NOT WORTHY

Definition:

Our own false belief system that we aren't good enough. It's a low self-esteem issue.

Unwanted Consequence:

You create relationships, often abusive, that match your expectations of not being "good enough."

3. TRUST AND "AWFULIZING" OUR ASSUMPTIONS

Definition:

Expecting the worst in others and from life, anticipating the time when the other person will "mess up."

Unwanted Consequence:

We usually create relationships that mirror our expectations of this world. If you view relationships as unsafe and unworthy of our trust, that is what you will eventually receive.

Fear often results from a commitment to become healthier and break old habits. Our subconscious naturally seeks the familiarity of old patterns and old belief systems. But by taking one small, sustainable step every day to live our new lives by **choice** rather than by **chance** or by **habit**, we can begin to make the changes necessary to create what we desire and deserve.

Dick Sutphen, author of *Enlightenment Transcripts,* provides this strategy for managing fear. When you feel afraid, ask yourself:

- What am I afraid of?
- Is it real or perceived?
- What's the payoff for having this fear?
- If the fear is perceived rather than real, what can I do and what am I willing to do to break the pattern?

Answering those questions can help you sort things out nicely. If the fear is real, take action. Otherwise, recognize it for what it is.

The Greatest Remorse — Unexpressed Love?

"Freedom is what you do
with what's been done to you."
Jean-Paul Sartre

At one time or another, nearly all of us have lamented a lost love. Maybe looked back with regret at things we wish we had said or done. *I couldn't express love when I had the chance and now it's too late.* The cause of that lost opportunity is often fear.

Yet fear also can be the beginning point of our greatest growth. It's been said that life begins "at the edge of our comfort zone." In our journey to becoming whole, hidden fears will always arise. It's a natural defense mechanism. It's an attempt to resist change. *Don't let it win!*

Change can be uncomfortable and even frightening at times, particularly in the beginning. But if you hold tight to your commitment and the journey to receive the abundant gifts that life wants to give you, success will be yours. By making a plan to do one thing each week toward your journey, you will begin to experience an exhilaration that few people ever do.

One of our biggest obstacles is a fear of conflict with others. This fear can reflect any number of conditioning patterns we receive from our parents or other caregivers in the first years of our lives. *Do what I say. Play nice. Be good.* Don't let this fear control you. Once you're willing to face it, you truly begin to grow into the person you want to become, the person who attracts a Soul Mate to you.

NOTES:

Overview of Key Concepts and Ideas

- There are three relationship patterns: Denial, Indulgence, and Integrity.
- There are three universal fears: Abandonment/Separation, Not Worthy, and Lack of Trust.
- There are two basic emotions: Love and Fear.
- The greatest remorse is Unexpressed Love.

Four-Step Action Plan

1. Identify where you are running patterns of Denial or Indulgence. Set goals for changing the patterns and celebrate when you do.
2. Acknowledge when you run the pattern of Integrity. Celebrate the positive effect it has on your life.
3. Be aware of how you may be feeding fear in your life. Are you feeding it or making it your ally?
4. Learn and practice healthy conflict-resolution skills with others.

> "One's mind, once stretched by a new idea,
> never regains its original dimensions."
> *Oliver Wendell Holmes*

CHAPTER EIGHT

UNDERSTANDING BOUNDARIES AND HOW TO ESTABLISH THEM

"If you can learn from hard knocks,
you can also learn from soft touches."

Carolyn Kenmore

Soul Mate relationships are about love, awareness, trust, and sharing. So you may wonder what a chapter on establishing boundaries is doing in this book.

We all have emotional boundaries that must not be violated. Violating another's boundaries is the prime cause of conflict in any relationship. Understanding your boundaries and being clear about them with your partner will help you handle conflict appropriately when it arises – and it does, even among Soul Mates! Practicing "the art of love in conflict" – replacing anger and fear with understanding and respect – will be an important part of your journey.

I have never read a more powerful illustration of the humbling power of love over fear than in the story that follows.

The train clanked and rattled through the suburbs of Tokyo on a drowsy spring afternoon. Our car was comparatively empty — few housewives with their kids in tow, some old folks going shopping. I gazed absently at the drab houses and dusty hedgerows.

At one station the doors opened and, suddenly, the afternoon quiet was shattered by a man bellowing violent, incomprehensible curses. The man staggered into our car. He wore laborer's clothing and was big, drunk, and dirty. Screaming, he swung at a woman holding a baby. The blow sent her spinning into the laps of an elderly couple. It was a miracle that the baby was unharmed.

Terrified, the couple jumped up and scrambled toward the other end of the car. The laborer aimed a kick at the retreating back of the old woman but missed as she scuttled to safety. This so enraged the drunk that he grabbed the metal pole in the center of the car and tried to wrench it out of its stanchion. I could see that one of his hands was cut and bleeding. The train lurched ahead, the passengers frozen with fear. I stood up.

I was young then, some 20 years ago, and in pretty good shape. I'd been putting in a solid eight hours of Aikido training nearly every day for the past three years. I liked to throw and grapple. I thought I was tough. The trouble was, my martial skill was untested in actual combat. As students of Aikido, we were not allowed to fight.

"Aikido," my teacher has said again and again, "is the art of reconciliation. Whoever has the mind to fight has broken his connection with the universe. If you try to dominate people, you're

already defeated. We study how to resolve conflict, not how to start it."

I listened to his words. I tried hard. I even went so far as to cross the street to avoid the "chimpira," the pinball punks who lounged around the train station. My forbearance exalted me. I felt both tough and holy. In my heart, however, I wanted an absolute legitimate opportunity whereby I might save the innocent by destroying the guilty.

"This is it!" I said to myself as I got to my feet. "People are in danger. If I don't do something fast, somebody will probably get hurt."

Seeing me stand up, the drunk recognized a chance to focus his rage. "Aha!" he roared. "A foreigner! You need a lesson in Japanese manners!"

I held on tightly to the commuter strap overhead and gave him a slow look of disgust and dismissal. I planned to take this turkey apart, but he had to make the first move. I wanted him mad, so I pursed my lips and blew him an insolent kiss.

"All right!" he hollered. "You're gonna get a lesson!" He gathered himself for a rush at me.

A fraction of a second before he could move, someone shouted, "Hey!" It was earsplitting. I remember the strangely joyous, lilting quality of it — as though you and a friend had been searching diligently for something, and he had suddenly stumbled upon it. "Hey!"

I wheeled to my left; the drunk spun to his right. We both stared down at a little old Japanese man. He must have been well into his seventies, this tiny gentleman, sitting there in his kimono. He took no notice of me, but beamed delightedly at the laborer, as though he had a most important, most welcome secret to share.

"C'mere," the old man said in an easy vernacular, beckoning to the drunk. "C'mere and talk with me." He waved his hands lightly.

The big man followed, as if on a string. He planted his feet belligerently in front of the old gentleman and roared above the clacking wheels. "Why should I talk to you?" The drunk now had his back to me. If his elbow moves so much as a millimeter, I'd drop him in his socks.

The old man continued to beam at the laborer. "What'cha been drinkin'?" he asked, his eyes sparkling with interest. "I been drinkin' sake," the laborer bellowed back, "and it's none of your business!" Flecks of spittle spattered the old man.

"Oh, that's wonderful," the old man said, "absolutely wonderful! You see, I love sake, too. Every night me and my wife, (she's 76, you know), we warm up a little bottle of sake and take it out into the garden, and we sit on an old wooden bench. We watch the sun go down, and we look to see how our persimmon tree is doing. My great-grandfather planted that tree, and we worry about whether it will recover from those ice storms we had last winter. Our tree has done better than I expected, though, especially when you consider the poor quality of the soil. It is gratifying to watch when we take our sake and go out to enjoy the evening — even when it rains!" He looked at the laborer, eyes twinkling.

As he struggled to follow the old man, his face began to soften. His fists slowly unclenched. "Yeah," he said, "I love persimmons, too ... " his voice trailed off.

"Yes," said the old man, smiling, "and I'm sure you have a wonderful wife."

"No," replied the laborer. "My wife died." Very gently, swaying *with the motion of the train, the big man began to sob. "I don't got no wife, I don't got no home, I don't got no job. I'm so ashamed of myself." Tears rolled down his cheeks, a spasm of despair rippled through his body.*

As I stood there in my well-scrubbed youthful innocence, my make-this-world-safe-for-democracy righteousness, I felt dirtier than he was.

Then the train arrived at my stop. As the doors opened, I heard the old man cluck sympathetically. "My, my," he said, "that is a difficult predicament indeed. Sit down here and tell me about it."

I turned my head for one last look. The laborer was sprawled on the seat with his head in the old man's lap. The old man was softly stroking the filthy, matted hair.

As the train pulled away, I sat down on a bench in the station. What I had wanted to do with muscle had been accomplished with kind words. I had just seen Aikido in action, and the essence of it was love. I would have to practice the art with an entirely different spirit. It would be a long time before I could speak about the resolution of conflict.

(Used with permission of Riki Moss and the Estate of Terry Dobson.)

Seven Additional Pointers on Boundaries and Conflict

1. **Understand your own history and reactions.**
   We all have relationship patterns that either support or don't support us in achieving our goals. By acknowledging them and creating a plan to change our negative patterns, we open the door for growth. The Spanish poet Juan Ramon Jimenez

said, "I cannot believe how much of my creativity I have used to push life and people away." When we choose to remain unaware of our negative patterns and not own our history, we push life and people away.

2. **Deal appropriately with conflicts.**
Take the time to learn how to deal with conflict peacefully and respectfully. When we educate ourselves on how to resolve uncomfortable interactions, we provide the space for creating a clear and clean relationship with others.

3. **Remember that "No" is a complete sentence.**
Self-explanatory!

4. **Set and visualize measurable goals for change.**
Identifying your goals and setting timeframes for accomplishment will help you make the greatest and fastest progress.

5. **See your relationships as mirrors.**
Our outer world is a direct reflection of what we feel and believe about ourselves internally. Use your experiences to show you where you need to do your work and where you have done your work. Keep out the blame and judgment. It's important to love yourself into change instead of trying to beat yourself into submission. Life can be painful, but suffering is optional.

6. **Set a direction and stay unattached to the outcome.**
Set your goals and then watch what shows up! Practice not letting events on the outside determine how you feel about

yourself. Learning to trust that all things work together for the good is a positive step toward building a life full of peace, joy, and trust. Only when we truly begin to trust ourselves, can we learn how to live fully.

7. **Network with others for support.**
Connecting with people who are on a similar path of self-discovery and learning can provide you with much encouragement as you grow in your life. Consider limiting your exposure to people in your life who are negative or don't share similar values.

NOTES:

Overview of Key Concepts and Ideas

- We have two responses to conflict: Love or Fear.
- Educating ourselves on how to handle conflict appropriately lays the framework for healthy interactions. ·
- Experiences that appear in our lives show us where we have done our work and where we need to do more work.

Four-Step Action Plan

1. Observe others who practice the art of love in conflict.
2. Identify how you can incorporate these strategies in your own relationship interactions.
3. Understand your boundaries and set them with others.
4. Learn, develop, and enhance your conflict-resolution skills.

Part II

SHARED COMMUNICATIONS

CONCLUSION

You have now learned the foundational and awareness principles needed to begin creating space for **Shared Communications** with a partner.

It's important to remember at this point that all of us have beliefs that serve us and beliefs that don't. When you begin to approach life as an opportunity to grow and choose to make the necessary changes (while uncovering bits and pieces of yourself), it can become a miraculous and joyful journey. As Thomas Merton said, *"Life is not a problem to be solved, but a mystery to be lived."*

This world of self-exploration is only for the courageous of heart — loving is risky. But, then, "all of life is the exercise of risk," as William Sloan Coffin has pointed out.

What awaits you on the other side is the possibility of living your dreams. Take the chance!

SUMMARY

The Components of Shared Communication

- Understanding that your major relationship belief systems are created in the first six years of life.

- Many of your strongest beliefs reside on the unconscious level.

- Your beliefs about life and relationships create your day-to-day experiences.

- Everyone is attracted to others based on unhealed wounds from childhood. Therefore, you unconsciously choose partners who have similar wounds so they can help you heal.

- Bringing your unconscious intentions to conscious awareness will allow you to live your life by choice, not chance.

- There are six powerful strategies for recognizing and changing outdated beliefs.

- Affirmations are a way of reinforcing positive beliefs while beginning the process of changing negative ones.

- The Soul Mate Affirmation can help build your faith and reinforce possibility. Say it twice a day.

- The "Yeah, but" Family of thoughts limits our ability to manifest our dreams.

- There are three relationship patterns: Denial, Indulgence, and Integrity. When we run a negative pattern, we make it stronger.

- Two basic emotions drive us: Love and Fear.

- There are three universal fears: Abandonment/Separation, Not Worthy, and Surrender/Trust.

- Most of our fears are of the future.

- The greatest remorse is Unexpressed Love.

- Setting boundaries and knowing how to deal with conflict appropriately are the keys to maintaining a healthy relationship.

PART III

AFFINITY

The Third Foundational Key

"They live in wisdom who see themselves
in all and all in them."
Bhagavad-Gita

Affinity

CHAPTER NINE

THE CYCLE OF RELATIONSHIPS

"It is good to have an end to journey towards;
but it is the journey that matters, in the end."
Ursula K. LeGuin

If you ever find yourself in a relationship with someone you might love but at the same time don't actually **like** — the warning bells should be going off. There's a big difference between the two! Liking and feeling a kinship with your partner — **affinity** — is an absolute given in a Soul Mate relationship.

Affinity is about making the effort to discover who a potential partner really is on many levels and making sure these answers align with where you're going in your life. It helps if he or she is the kind of person you would want to be yourself and displays attributes you desire. In a sense, your Soul Mate is your best friend.

So many times, though, it's difficult to see whether you really like someone or whether you're just lonely and want to be in a relationship. A good way to sort through the confusion is to ask yourself: *"If there were only one person with whom I could share the rest of my life and no one else existed, would I choose this person?"* If the answer is "no" or "I'm not sure," you need to reexamine your choice.

Making Discriminating Choices

"Learning is not attained by chance.
It must be sought for with ardor
and attended to with diligence."
Abigail Adams

Relationships go through four distinct phases, and learning about them will help you make better choices in partners. You'll understand why you feel a certain way at a certain time and whether that feeling is love or something else.

The Relationship Cycle

Introduction

Expansion

Attraction   Magnetism
Bliss   Romantic
Hope   Ecstasy
Possibility   Excitement

*Suspended Judgment

Actualized Love

Growth   Joy
Harmony   Aliveness
Creativity   Co-Commitment
Compassion   Connection

Re-expansion

Self-Awareness   Confusion
Decisions   Skills
Openness   Practice
Resolving   Changing

*Awareness of Choices

Contraction

Power Struggle   Fear
Hypersensitivity   Frustration
Overly Judgmental   Effort/Work
Disillusionment   Anger

PHASE I – EXPANSION

"No snowflake ever falls on the wrong place."
Zen proverb

When you're eager to meet a special someone, your unconscious mind automatically turns into a matchmaker. At parties, the office, even on vacations, it constantly sizes up people who might match your belief systems about love. The unconscious mind is looking for someone who will help you heal your psychological wounds from the past, someone who can help put unresolved situations to rest.

And when you meet that special someone – look out! The brain triggers the production of PEA (Phenyl Ethylamine), an attraction chemical commonly referred to as the "Love Drug." It's nature's way of drawing two people together.

With PEA on the job, romance is in the air! You experience euphoria and can hardly wait to see the other person. PEA does away with pain and fear of intimacy; it actually makes you crave contact. The libido soars, and you begin to think it is normal to feel this way forever – and that it *will* last forever if this is "real love."

Beware! As good as it feels, this PEA-driven phase of the relationship cycle can derail even those who do find their Soul Mate.

This is called the **Expansion Phase** (also sometimes the Romantic Phase), and it's home to a glut of extraordinary sensations – bliss, magnetism, ecstasy, hope, illusions about the future, excitement, expectation, and openness. Sex is typically great. You may find yourself saying, "We stayed up all night talking" or "I have never felt this way before!"

It's the stage where your judgment about the relationship can be most distorted. Because it feels so good, we tend to ignore red flags and potential problems. This period is the most challenging for remaining conscious of your purpose and gathering information to make sure this person matches the criteria you're looking for in a Soul Mate.

The effect of the Love Drug begins to wear off within three to eighteen months. And the more contact you have, the more quickly PEA fades.

Quite often, people think that when PEA runs its course, they have "fallen out of love," but love is much more than a chemical reaction. Love is about behavior, integrity, authenticity, trust, respect, and vulnerability. It has a depth and a richness that far exceed the superficial attraction where the relationship began.

No matter how enthralling a potential Soul Mate might be, it's crucial not to let this normal physical process overshadow the need to really get to know each other before becoming sexually intimate. I recommend waiting until at least twelve dates — or even longer. (And breakfast, lunch, and dinner in one day do not count as three dates!)

When PEA is flowing, it's important to maintain emotional and mental awareness. Be patient and give yourself some time. It will be much the wiser choice in the long run. Waiting gives you enough time to make sure this person is someone you really would want to share intimate moments with and is also someone who can meet your long-term objectives. When you share your physical body with another person, you create an emotional connection that makes it harder to end the relationship, if you must.

Once PEA has run its course, the relationship moves to a new, very different phase. Many people don't like to think they have to work at romance or love, but in the second phase of the relationship, it becomes clear that they do. The Contraction Phase could be described as a character builder. It's a time when you're faced with contemplating your own fears and a time when relationship issues surface. And have no illusions about it: Issues *do* surface for everyone.

PHASE II – CONTRACTION

"In the middle of difficulty lies opportunity."

Albert Einstein

Once PEA wears off, anxieties about love and being in an intimate relationship naturally arise. Unhealed wounds and fears from the past take the place of unfettered bliss. This is typically a time of disillusion, frustration, power struggles, and puzzlement: *What happened?* Many relationships stall at this point. But by recognizing that this is a normal progression, potentially well-matched partners can move forward and keep their relationship vibrantly growing.

During this period, unresolved issues from previous relationships have the power to derail even the most promising relationship. It may be a lack of forgiveness or repressed anger involving earlier partners, given new life because of its similarity to a situation that arises with the new relationship. These issues arouse our deepest fears. All too often we begin to project our unresolved emotions onto our partner and start to destroy the relationship. Only by **letting go of the past** can you truly be happy with the present and receive the gift of a loving future.

Confronting your feelings about past experiences will allow you to move forward. Use the worksheet below to revisit relationships and the emotions you now attach to them. Do people from your past – parents, siblings, past loves, etc. – bring forth feelings of anger, regret, or disappointment? Write as many names as you can recall and list any unforgiven past hurt. In other words, list the ways your body and mind tell you there is significant unfinished business with this person.

LETTING GO OF THE PAST

Person

_____

Unforgiven Past Hurt

_____

_____

_____

Person

_____

Unforgiven Past Hurt

_____

_____

_____

Person

_____

Unforgiven Past Hurt

_____

_____

_____

Person

_____

Unforgiven Past Hurt

_____

_____

_____

Person

_____

Unforgiven Past Hurt

_____

_____

_____

Now, let's begin the healing. List these same people again, but this time think back and identify lessons you learned from them. **Keep it positive.** What did they teach you? One example could be that you learned how to draw boundaries with others. Another could be that you learned to laugh and play like a child or to be sexually explorative. By identifying what each person added to your life, the process of healing and letting go can begin.

Person

_____

Lesson Learned

_____

_____

_____

Person

_____

Lesson Learned

_____

_____

_____

Person

_____

Lesson Learned

_____

_____

_____

Person

_____

Lesson Learned

_____

_____

_____

Person

_____

Lesson Learned

_____

_____

_____

In *Illusions,* Richard Bach's follow-up book to *Jonathan Livingston Seagull,* the author writes, "We draw problems into our life because we need their gifts." We all draw others into our path so we can learn through the experience. What you choose to do with that experience is your choice. Do you choose to magnify and harbor the pain or do you look for the positive lesson you learned? It's your choice. There are no victims unless you choose that for yourself.

When we haven't healed our hurts and anger from the past, we can end up with what Angeles Arrien, an expert on native spirituality, calls the "haunting of relationships." Instead of two people in a relationship, there can be as many as half a dozen uninvited "ghosts" fighting for attention!

If your past is haunting your present and threatening to destroy all that is good, a guided imagery visualization is an effective technique for laying those ghosts to rest. Here's a simple and effective visualization designed to help you forgive and get on with your life.

A Simple Visualization

> "Even a thought, even a possibility,
> can shatter us and transform us."
>
> *Friedrich Nietzsche*

Sit in a quiet place and close your eyes. Breathe in and out deeply, giving your mind and body time to relax and refocus. Now, imagine you are walking on a wooded path. You come upon a cottage that seems to welcome you. Two steps lead up to the front door. A sign on the door says "Safety and Reassurance." You know this door leads to a place where you can safely practice forgiveness. You can come here anytime, whenever you need it.

As you open the door, you see beautiful pictures on the walls. They remind you of the happiest times in your life. You notice a door off to the right. It leads to a room where you will be able to experience healthy forgiveness and closure with anyone from your past. And once you experience that closure, you can move forward in the present and into the future without any haunting from the past.

As you enter this room, you see one of the people on your list. As this person stands before you, you feel no anger. You learned some positive lessons from this person that life wanted you to learn. It was all for the best. You begin talking with this person about the positive side of those experiences. This person encourages you to continue talking as you describe the lessons and gifts you gained from the relationship. There is nothing to fear. You now hear yourself say, "You are forgiven." The haunting influence from your past is over.

Now imagine cutting all energy cords that connect you to that person. The past no longer connects to your present. You stand in front of that person, free from any past experience. Lovingly but firmly, you say goodbye in a way that brings resolution. Then you watch that person turn and leave.

Return to the front door and open it. Walk down the steps and continue on down the wooded path. You know that anytime you need to bring a healthy closure to any relationship, the cottage exists for you. Take two deep breaths and return to the present. Life is now yours to live to the fullest, no longer burdened by the pain of yesterday.

Sometimes after doing a forgiveness exercise with someone, old memories of hurt may continue to surface. My young nephew coined his own phrase for this: "He jumped right back in my head!" A strategy I use to reinforce the forgiveness process when "someone jumps back in my head" is to think of that person and say, "May you be filled with love and kindness; may you be filled with peace." Repeating these phrases helps begin the process of "reprogramming" the mental computer so it doesn't focus on the old feelings of pain. It allows us to magnify the lessons we've learned and not to stay stuck in the past.

Depending on the depth of hurt or disappointment you've experienced, forgiveness may take time. It will happen. Give yourself time and stay positive. Be kind and gently work to free yourself from the past. Freedom and healing are yours to claim if you open your soul to the relationship's gifts instead of the pain.

Forgiving others is good for the soul; so is forgiving yourself. We all have looked back with regret at hurtful things we said or did that emotionally harmed others. This unforgiven self-recrimination serves no healthy purpose.

You can take control of your ghosts through a process of conscious self-forgiveness. Here's a simple strategy I personally use. It begins with my "owning" the hurtful behavior I exhibited. Then I identify the lesson I learned from that experience. And finally I set a vision for the future by stating:

"Next time I will _____."

Now, take a few moments and list events for which you need to forgive yourself.

Event: _____

_____

I own: _____

_____

Lesson I learned: _____

_____

Next time, I will: _____

_____

It can be tough to free yourself from feelings of guilt and remorse, but self-forgiveness is essential if you are to develop healthy relationships during the rest of your life.

It's time to return to the "cottage in the woods," to accept your own gift of forgiveness. As in the previous visualization, start by closing your eyes, taking several deep breaths, and totally relaxing. This time, visualize yourself in the hallway entrance. To your left is a door with a sign that reads, "The Self-Forgiveness Room." You know you can enter this room any time, now or in the future, when you feel the need. It will always be available. Today, it beckons you to enter. It has wanted you to enter for a long time.

You open the door and walk in. The only object you see is a large mirror in the center of the room, and you can feel it drawing you to look into it. It wills you to see the love in your heart — the love that guilt has tried to prevent you from seeing. Look deeply into the mirror and gently say, "I am forgiven." With those words, your reflection fills with joy; your soul is smiling at you. Yesterday's burdens have lifted, and joy floods your being. Your soul soars, like that of a child who feels protected, loved, and safe. There's a new smile on your face, and you can feel it in your heart.

Rejoice: *You* are forgiven. It is a new day, a new beginning. The future is bright if you will accept what it has to offer. You are free to love *yourself,* as well as others.

Guilt Trip Times Two

My friend Bob married for the first time when he was twenty-one. The marriage lasted ten years, and toward the end divorce had becomes inevitable. As a couple, they were exhausted. Bob took the first step toward ending the relationship by leaving Theresa.

Two years after the divorce, still emotionally on the rebound, Bob wed a second time. He was trying to recapture what he had lost, but this marriage lasted just eight months.

Bob's guilt intensified. He never forgave himself for the two failed marriages, and the wounds from those experiences were still haunting him when he began dating Susan a year later.

Susan had never been married, and she was growing very much in love with Bob. She liked his gentle ways and his caring heart, and she knew her mom and dad would, too, when they met him for the first time at Christmas. "I wonder what my dad will say when he finds out that I could be wife number three someday?" Susan teased lightly.

Bob's reply was an arctic shockwave. With hurt and embarrassment in his voice, he said he was sorry she would have to deal with that problem. He said he would never want anyone to have to share his pain. He apologized for creating such a difficult situation for her. The pent-up hurt in his heart had prevented him from seeing that Susan would never hurt him intentionally. He had heard not an innocent joke, but an indictment.

Despite the bitter words, Susan knew Bob wasn't angry with her. And what she said in return changed his life. Taking Bob's hand, she told him what he meant to her. "Don't you understand? I love the Bob that you are. And if you hadn't gone through all that you have gone through, you wouldn't be you. Who you are is a gift of everything in life that you have gone through and experienced. Your experiences have made you perfect for me. Don't ever apologize for what you have gone through. It's what molded you into who you are today. And that is the person I am falling in love with."

Susan's understanding gave Bob a sense of freedom he had not felt in years. It freed him to love himself again. It freed him to view the painful experiences of his life through a different filter — not of guilt but of the lessons they had taught him. No longer would he let guilt interfere with the joy that life wanted to give him.

Life can begin anew for you, too. You can forgive yourself. It's a choice only you can make. No matter what you've experienced in the past, you can choose to free yourself from all bondage. You can stop those negative influences from causing any more destruction in your life.

As Bob learned, you are who you are because of all that you have gone through. Everything that has happened in your life's journey molds the person you are and the person you will become — the ideal partner for a Soul Mate. You must forgive yourself. It's not an option — it's a requirement — if you want to continue the journey of finding the *best* that life has to offer *you*. Don't settle for less.

Forgiveness is powerful medicine, and it's yours to choose. With it, you can fully experience the joy of the gifts of today. It's the first step to wholeness, and it's ultimately essential to the sustenance of a successful Soul Mate relationship. Don't delay your journey. **Forgiving yourself can start today.**

PHASE III – RE-EXPANSION

"You can have anything you want
if you want it desperately enough.
You must want it with an exuberance
that erupts through the skin and joins the energy
that created the world."

Sheila Braham

We are unconsciously attracted to people who appear to be good candidates for helping us heal the wounds of earlier relationships. But couples who bring unfinished business from the past into their new relationships tend to have the same predictable results. The old frustrations, anger, and disillusionment about love bubble up anew.

The message here is that if you don't acknowledge and heal those old wounds, they will cause you pain forever. That's why many potentially good relationships run aground in Phase II of the relationship cycle. These sadder-but-no-wiser individuals often move from one relationship to another and another, and their pain and hurt continue to thwart any long-term future happiness.

We must heal ourselves first, and the key to this healing is *consciousness* – for both partners. The two of you need to *consciously* work together in respect, trust, and integrity to choose what steps to take in your healing process. The Re-expansion, or Awareness, Phase begins when both you and your partner are emotionally and mentally aware of your own imperfections and your emotional baggage, and you consciously choose to love and encourage each other as you work to heal together.

Now is a good time to examine your previous relationships. If you're currently in a relationship, change the statements to the present. These five questions are designed to help you stay on track toward developing a Soul Mate relationship.

1. What did you and your partner or partners argue or disagree about most? What were the sources of conflict? Think about how these issues began and repeated themselves and try to identify what belief systems might have been responsible.

    _____

    _____

    _____

    _____

    _____

2. Unresolved fears and anger resulting from failed relationships are the ruin of many a promising romance. In what ways have you projected potentially damaging issues from the past into a succeeding relationship?

    _____

    _____

    _____

    _____

    _____

3. In past relationships, how did you lovingly communicate in a way that your partner could hear you? How will you do this in the future?

_____

_____

_____

_____

_____

4. Some people find professional counseling helpful during this phase of the relationship cycle. If you were to consider counseling in the future, what specific issues would you seek assistance with?

_____

_____

_____

_____

_____

5. There are a number of excellent books on the dynamics that exist in relationships. (Check the Recommended Reading List at the back of this book.) List three books you intend to read.

Book 1: _____

Book 2: _____

Book 3: _____

> "For in truth great love is born
> of great knowledge of the thing loved."
> *Leonardo da Vinci*

The Re-expansion Phase is a time of growth and change. Partners committed to the healing process begin a journey of self-awareness by practicing relationship skills that are designed to put to rest old wounds from the past. During this time, you must be open to learn more about yourself, not just about your partner, and both of you must be willing to change.

This commitment to growth, and then the actual moving forward, is an exciting milepost in a relationship. It may not be an easy time, because you will need to educate yourself on how to be a healthy partner. This may require attending workshops on conflict resolution, improving communications techniques, listening effectively, or learning how to set healthy boundaries.

Start this new phase with a meeting of minds. Have a conversation with your partner about his or her behaviors – which are healthy for the relationship, which are unhealthy? This can be a powerful beginning if you're loving and kind. Don't be accusatory! When you talk about hurtful behaviors in the relationship, tell your partner why it hurts you and focus on the way it makes you feel – for example, sad, physically ill, or heartsick. Hold both yourself and your partner accountable when addressing a grievance. Don't focus on *their* insensitivity but on how this perceived hurt made *you* feel. This is the healthy, loving way to resolve conflicts – the respect, trust, and love you demonstrate will only make your relationship grow closer.

As you begin to apply these new ways of thinking, it obviously won't feel natural. In fact, it may be difficult to keep your focus at first and you may become confused. That's actually a positive sign. As Neale Donald Walsch writes in *Friendship with God,* "Confusion is the first step toward wisdom."

PHASE IV – ACTUALIZED LOVE

People who have given up hope of ever finding their Soul Mates are the most tragic figures I encounter in my work. I've heard a lot of sad excuses. "I'm too old to find someone" is a common one. Others lament, "I had a Soul Mate (as if there is only one!), but I destroyed what could have been a wonderful relationship through my own ignorance." And perhaps the most common one I hear is, "I missed my Soul Mate because I wasn't ready, and now they're married to someone else."

This is so unfortunate! Such hopelessness is totally unfounded. If you are one of those people who resign themselves to the "fate" of never achieving a Soul Mate relationship, you may be unconsciously trying to maintain your dysfunctional role as "victim." Wake up to the fact that the universe is full of potential Soul Mates, and the only limitation is a closed mind. Open it to what great gifts are in store for you.

"Opportunity, for most of us, doesn't knock just once:
she raps a continual tattoo on our doors.
The pity is that much of the time,
we're either too preoccupied to hear,
or too lethargic to answer."

Benjamin J. Fairless

Actualized Love is another name for Soul Mate love. This is a relationship between two people that encompasses spiritual, mental, physical, and emotional growth. It's a deep, binding, mutually rewarding love that affects not only you and your partner, but everyone your lives touch.

But this is no time to rest on your laurels! Soul Mates are "aware" partners who actively nurture their relationship through good and bad times. Through my own experiences in a Soul Mate relationship and learning from other Soul Mate couples, I can tell you that these relationships bring feelings of harmony, joy, and compassion; they're a catalyst for creativity; they foster mutual commitment.

No couple in the world agrees on everything all the time – nor should they. But such conflicts that do arise in a Soul Mate relationship tend to be minor and resolved in a way that preserves the trust and high regard the partners feel for one another. Not only do Soul Mates choose to love each other, they choose to cherish all that their partner is and will become.

Soul Mate journeys aren't perfect; they are the journeys of two people who share a desire to help and nurture each other through thick and thin. When storm clouds start to gather, they don't let anger blind them to their true feelings of deep affection. During times of conflict, my Soul Mate and I usually find ourselves asking, "How can I support you?" Later, we explore what went wrong and ask ourselves, "What can we do so this doesn't happen again?" This approach sends your partner an affirming signal that you want the best for both of you, and it also has the effect of "problem-solving" for the future.

Soul Mate relationships are created when two individuals commit themselves to creating the richest love relationship possible. One person cannot do it alone. Each partner makes a conscious decision to love, cherish, and adore (all three!) the other. The result is a joyful life that you and every other human being deserves and can have.

All "conscious" relationships give you a way to see yourself more clearly. By consciously understanding your foremost desires and committing yourself to personal growth from this day forward, you begin laying the foundation for experiencing Soul Mate love. Remember: The journey to finding your Soul Mate always begins with yourself.

NOTES:

Overview of Key Concepts and Ideas

- Relationships cycle through four phases.
- In Phase I (Expansion), your body produces an attraction chemical, the endorphin PEA, also known as the Love Drug.
- During Phase I, it's imperative that you stay vigilant to any "red flags" about a partner's long-term suitability.
- In Phase II (Contraction), the attraction chemical has worn off and all of your unresolved fears and unhealed wounds from the past show up.
- Practicing forgiveness is one way to free yourself from the hurts of the past.
- In Phase III, (Re-expansion), you and your partner begin to apply healthy relationship behaviors, resolve old conflicts, learn new skills for increased understanding, and become open to self-awareness patterns.
- In Phase IV (Actualized Love), you and your partner have consciously made the decision to commit to a Soul Mate relationship, a journey that is characterized by growth, joy, harmony, creativity, connection, commitment, compassion, and very little conflict.

Six-Step Action Plan

1. During Phase I, stay awake and aware, and ask questions of your potential partner.
2. Use your *"Designing Your Own Soul Mate"* list to make sure your potential partner is appropriate for where you're going in your life.
3. Begin learning and applying healthy relationship skills and

awareness in your life.

4. Set a goal to learn one new relationship skill a month for six months. Acknowledge your progress and celebrate when you apply a new skill.

5. Read books and attend workshops to learn how to use healthy behaviors in intimate relationships.

6. Remember that slow, continual progress lays the foundation for Soul Mate love. Don't get impatient. Love the journey! As Mother Teresa said, "Do small things with great love."

NOTES:

Part III

AFFINITY

CONCLUSION

Affinity is the foundational principle for conscious awareness within our relationships. As you move through the cycles and patterns of a relationship, understanding this principle will help you make wiser choices in potential and long-term partners.

In this section of the book, you learned about the physical and mental components (PEA and the four phases of the relationship cycle) that play major roles in our attraction to potential romantic partners. Fully understanding these components provides a wonderful opportunity for exploring your own level of growth and discovering areas that still need to be evaluated.

FINDING
YOUR SOUL MATE™
HANDBOOK

SUMMARY

"In my life's chain of events, nothing was accidental.
Everything happened according to an inner need."

Hannah Senesh

Change is never easy. But the journey toward Soul Mate love doesn't lie in the traditional. It lies in the hands of those who consciously choose to challenge their fears and past hurts, accept forgiveness, learn significant relationship skills, and accept nothing less than the best of what life has to offer.

How fast life goes by. It's nothing less than a tragedy when we continue on an unconscious path, awash in fears, never healing, never really knowing how to love and be loved. The gifts that are available to us are magnificent, if we will just open our minds and our hearts.

The journey to a Soul Mate relationship is an exhilarating, lifelong adventure. It won't always be easy. Progress always takes effort and concentration. Remember that real progress starts not with your partner adapting to you, but with you doing the work necessary to heal your own wounds.

Stay focused. Life's best is but a small journey down the road. It's up to you to take the first step.

> "I always knew that one day
> I would take this road, but
> Yesterday I did not know
> Today would be the day."
>
> *Nagurjuna*

SEVEN MYTHS ABOUT SOUL MATES

You can't believe everything you've read or heard about Soul Mate relationships. Here are seven of the most common myths.

Myth 1   There is only one Soul Mate for each person.

Not at all. In your lifetime, many people could prove to be a suitable Soul Mate match for you. The reason is that we tend to attract people toward us in relationships who mirror where we are in our growth at a particular point. As you grow, you can – and probably will – attract others.

Myth 2   When my Soul Mate appears, I won't have to handle any more relationship challenges.

Even Soul Mate relationships must be consciously nurtured. When two people are committed to consciously supporting one another, there is typically more harmony, joy, sharing, compassion, and minimal conflict. But you have to be realistic — life still throws you a challenge once in a while. When you are consciously aware, relationships help you see where your own healing work is needed.

Myth 3   It's destiny! Soul Mates are destined to be ... or not to be.

Everyone creates his and her own destiny. Our experiences of life — joy, love, and relationships — are determined by our choices and attitudes. *Illusions* author Richard Bach hit the nail on the head when he said, *"We draw people into our life. What we do with them is our choice."* A potentially good relationship can be destroyed if one, or both, partners are not emotionally healthy.

Myth 4   You can't fight your fate. If a relationship is destined to be, it will be, in whatever form it happens to be. Accept it and be happy, even if it's not that much fun.

Life is painful, but suffering is optional. It's all too easy to turn a relationship into a masochistic disaster by believing that "If I'm not struggling, then it must not be right." That's especially true if you're conditioned to believe that relationships are hard work. Having a Soul Mate relationship doesn't guarantee there won't be bumps in the road, but typically there is much joy, happiness, passion, and growth.

Myth 5   Being strongly attracted to someone is a sure way to know this person is a Soul Mate.

Sorry, but that may just be the chemicals talking. When we meet someone who seems to be a gift from heaven, our bodies produce an attraction chemical called Phenyl Ethylamine, or PEA, that gives us a natural high — and it can last quite a long time! PEA is nature's way of bringing people together for some obvious biological reasons. It can spin its spell for as long as a year and a half, clouding your judgment about your charming companion's actual long-term compatibility.

Myth 6   My Soul Mate can fulfill all of my emotional needs.

Whether you have a Soul Mate relationship or not, you're the only one who can be responsible for the way you think and feel. It's up to you to do what it takes every day to create and maintain emotional balance and stability in your life. To quote Joseph Campbell, *"You've got to find the Source inside you."*

Myth 7   Communication between Soul Mates is always easy.

You're only human, and that means you still have to work at Soul Mate relationships. Successful couples rely on strategies that lead to a resolution to misunderstandings or differences and preserve their respect, trust and integrity for one another.

"AM I TOO PICKY?"
And Other Commonly Asked Questions

<u>SHARED REALITY</u>

How do I know if I have the "right" purpose for my life and relationships?

Only you can decide what purpose is appropriate for your life. Sometimes our focus on "perfection" or getting it "just right" stymies the motivation to even begin. Just start somewhere — even if your purpose is "to be a more loving person." As you continue to do your healing work, you may find that other pieces of the puzzle fall into place.

How detailed should my *"Designing Your Own Soul Mate"* list be?

Make it as detailed as you can. Be sure to write down every last desire. This ensures you will be completely clear about what kind of person you're consciously interested in. The list will keep you focused as you meet potential partners.

My friends tell me I'm too picky. Could I be limiting myself by wanting way too much in a person?

There's a great saying that goes: *"It's a funny thing about life; if you refuse to accept anything but the best, you often get it!"* Go for it!

There is so much to remember. How do I not "fall back to sleep?"

Each month, choose one thing to do every day that will remind you of your dreams and goals. It could be as simple as expressing gratitude for the Soul Mate relationship of your dreams or repeating several times daily your Soul Mate affirmation. In the following months, choose a different type of reminder.

What's a first step I can take in determining if someone is a potential Soul Mate partner?

First, be completely clear about what you desire in a companion. Complete the *"Designing Your Own Soul Mate"* list and then identify your top six "non-negotiables." These are characteristics that a partner must possess, *no matter what!* Fashion questions around these non-negotiables and listen intently to the responses.

SHARED COMMUNICATIONS

I keep picking the same type of person over and over, even though I say I won't do this again. Why?

Our most powerful relationship belief systems lie in our unconscious. Because they initially feel comfortable or familiar, we repeat experiences we don't desire – even if they turn out to be painful. You can't just will yourself to change your belief systems. You need to create concrete, measurable strategies for changing those ingrained behaviors.

What is a first step to changing an undesirable belief?

Acknowledge it and own the belief. What shows up in your outer world is a direct reflection of what you believe in your inner world. Those things that repeatedly bring you what you don't want are life's way of saying, "Pay attention! This thing wants to be looked at and healed!" Then create a plan for changing your inner beliefs, so that your outer world can reflect your true desires.

Do beliefs really create our reality?

The beliefs you hold about yourself and about life are always reflected outwardly through the decisions and choices you make. People who live their lives "unconsciously" – rather than by choice and truth – experience a sense of being off track with their goals.

If I'm interested in someone who doesn't care about developing relationship skills, can it still work and grow into a Soul Mate relationship?

Yes, but only if you decide that this person's contribution to the relationship will be enough to keep you satisfied with your own life's journey. It's up to you to decide what "enough" is, and typically both partners in a Soul Mate relationship are very committed to mental, spiritual, emotional, and physical growth — both as a couple and as individuals.

Why do I hesitate to leave relationships I know aren't good for me?

People who settle for less in relationships typically worry that what they have is the best they can ever hope for! This is called "scarcity thinking," and it's based on fear. When fear takes over your decision-making, it's all too easy to settle for a BTN (Better Than Nothing) relationship. But as you begin to heal and come to realize — and believe — that the world is full of wonderful possibilities, it will become much easier to take care of yourself and move on when you need to.

I have a wonderful opportunity to work in another town, but my potential Soul Mate doesn't want to move. If I leave without him, am I missing out on the relationship of a lifetime?

One of the most regrettable fallacies about Soul Mates is that we're rationed to one per lifetime. That's simply not so. For each of us, there are many people who would be appropriate matches.

It's important to be true to yourself first. When you do that, relationships tend to fall into place. But if you let fear keep you where you are, you're not truly making a conscious choice — you're being held captive by that fear. By taking care of yourself first and honoring your needs, wonderful experiences tend to follow.

I feel like my last partner used me to get over his divorce. How can I forgive and move on?

It's not uncommon to become a "transformational healing object" when you allow yourself to get involved with someone who's fresh out of a relationship. It takes time for people to emotionally bring closure to a breakup. When you get involved with someone too soon, they may unconsciously associate you with the hurt and pain of that relationship. A powerful first step in letting go and moving forward would be to ask yourself: "What drew me toward this person? What was my opportunity for growth? What did I learn from this experience?" And, if a similar situation presents itself again, "What will I do differently?"

AFFINITY

I've fallen head-over-heels in love with several people, only to find out later we were incompatible. Now I realize it wasn't love and that I overlooked plenty of red flags! How can I become savvier in my choices?

When you first meet someone you're attracted to, it's all too easy to get lost in the possibility of what could be – because you're sure that this is the one! This emotional high is caused by an attraction chemical called PEA, and its effects can last for more than a year. But you can take control by establishing some firm boundaries for yourself. Such as committing to wait until you've had at least a dozen dates before considering intimacy. It's also a time when you need to ask lots of questions about this person's long-term goals and desires. Keep aware to the fact that PEA may be clouding your judgment and how easy it is to overlook potential red flags, such as undesirable patterns from past relationships that pop up again.

Do all relationships go through the four phases you talk about in the book?

Yes. How long a couple remains in any of the four phases of the relationship cycle depends on each person's healthiness and how willing they are to work together. It's possible, even, for couples who experience Soul Mate love to face issues going forward that bring their relationship back to an earlier phase.

If I don't feel a chemical attraction to another person, is there any hope for creating a Soul Mate relationship?

It's possible, if both of you are agreeable to that arrangement. However, my experience has been that partners may say it doesn't matter up-front, but down the road it does most of the time!

I know I'm jeopardizing the future of my relationship because of the way I act out on my fears. But what can I do?

The Contraction phase of a relationship is typically a time of fear and anxiety when many relationships are in danger of stalling. You can work your way through this period by first taking ownership of your undesirable behaviors — accepting what you are doing and why you are doing it and sharing those discoveries with your partner. Understanding what is driving your fears is the first step to making a commitment for positive change.

How can I not get discouraged when there's no Soul Mate on my radar screen?

One way is to realize that unless you can be happy with yourself, and also by yourself, you're not free to be extraordinarily happy with another person. Learning to create a life worth living, whether you're on your own or in a relationship, must be your foremost objective. After that, relationships tend to fall into place.

RECOMMENDED READING

Adrienne, Carol *The Purpose of Your Life Experiential Guide*

Arrien, Angeles *The Four-Fold Way: Walking the Paths of the Warrior, Teacher, Healer, and Visionary*

Bach, Richard *Illusions,*
The Bridge across Forever

Braden, Gregg *Walking between the Worlds*

Bryan, Mark with *The Artist's Way at Work*
Cameron, Julia, and
Allen, Catherine

Chopra, Deepak *The Seven Spiritual Laws of Success*

Cloud, Henry *Boundaries*

Cohen, Alan *The Dragon Doesn't Live Here Anymore*

Crenshaw, Theresa   *The Alchemy of Love and Lust*

De Angelis, Barbara   *Are You the One for Me?*

Dyer, Wayne   *Your Sacred Self,*
Real Magic,
You'll See It when You Believe It

Gawain, Shakti   *Living in the Light*

Gorski, Terence   *Getting Love Right*

Gottman, John   *Why Marriages Succeed or Fail*

Grabhorn, Lynn   *Excuse Me, Your Life is Waiting*

Hay, Louise   *You Can Heal Your Life*

Hendricks, Gaylord   *Conscious Loving*

Hendricks, Harville   *Getting the Love you Want,*
Keeping the Love You Find

Jampolsky, Gerald   *Love is Letting Go of Fear*

Jeffers, Susan   *Feel the Fear and Do It Anyway*

Jones, Laurie Beth   *The Path*

Lerner, Harriet   *The Dance of Intimacy,*
The Dance of Anger

Light, Phyllis   *Prince Charming Lives! (Princess Charming Does Too)*

Love, Patricia   *Hot Monogamy*

Millman, Dan   *Way of the Peaceful Warrior*

Sutphen, Dick   *Enlightenment Transcripts, The Master of Life Manual*

Tolle, Eckhart   *The Power of Now*

Vanzant, Iyanla   *One Day My Soul Just Opened Up, In the Meantime*

Walsch, Neale Donald *Conversations with God, Books I, II, and III, Friendship With God*

Welwood, John   *Journey of the Heart*

BIBLIOGRAPHY

Arrien, Angeles, *The Four-Fold Way™: Walking the Paths of the Warrior, Teacher, Healer, and Visionary.* San Francisco: HarperCollins, 1993. For further information, contact the office of Angeles Arrien, P.O. Box 2077, Sausalito, CA 94966; (415) 331-5050; www.angelesarrien.com.

Arrien, Angeles, *The Psychology of Shamanism.* Unit Three: Reclamation of the Soul: Shamanic Soul Retrieval Methods, Page 5. For the External Degree Program of the Institute of Transpersonal Psychology, Palo Alto, CA. Institute of Transpersonal Psychology, 1996.

Argyris, Chris, *Overcoming Organizational Defenses: Facilitating Organizational Learning.* Englewood Cliffs, NJ: Prentice-Hall, 1990.

Bach, Richard, *Illusions: The Adventures of a Reluctant Messiah.* New York: Dell Publishing, 1977.

Barks, Coleman with Moyne, John, *The Essential Rumi.* New York: Harper Collins, 1995.

Braden, Gregg, *Walking between the Worlds: The Science of Compassion.* Bellevue, WA: Radio Bookstore Press, 1997.

Bryan, Mark with Cameron, Julia and Allen, Catherine, *The Artist's Way at Work: Riding the Dragon, Twelve Weeks to Creative Freedom.* New York: William Morrow & Co., 1998.

Carroll, Lewis, *Alice's Adventures in Wonderland.* New York: Schocken Books, 1978.

Crenshaw, Theresa, *The Alchemy of Love & Lust: How our Sex Hormones Influence Our Relationships.* New York: Pocket Books, a division of Simon & Schuster, 1996.

De Angelis, Barbara, *Are You the One for Me? Knowing Who's Right & Avoiding Who's Wrong.* New York: Dell Publishing, 1992.

Grabhorn, Lynn, *Excuse Me, Your Life is Waiting: The Astonishing Power of Feelings.* Charlottesville, VA: Hampton Roads Publishing, 2000.

Hendricks, Gaylord and Kathlyn, *Conscious Loving: The Journey to Co-Commitment.* New York: Bantam Books, 1990

Hendricks, Harville, *Getting the Love You Want: A Guide for Couples.* New York: Harper & Row, 1988.

Hendricks, Harville, *Keeping the Love You Find: A Personal Guide.* New York: Pocket Books, 1992.

Kornfield, Jack, *The Roots of Buddhist Psychology* (six audiocassettes). Boulder, CO: Sounds True Inc., 1995

Sutphen, Dick, *Enlightenment Transcripts,* ©1986 Valley of the Sun Publishing, Box 38, Malibu, CA 90265, www.dicksutphen.com.

Walsch, Neale Donald, *Friendship with God: An Uncommon Dialogue* (six audiocassettes). San Bruno, CA: Audio Literature, 1999.

Walsch, Neale Donald, *Conversations with God: An Uncommon Dialogue, Book One.* Charlottesville, VA: Hampton Roads Publishing, 1995.

RESOURCE ACKNOWLEDGMENTS

The author extends a heartfelt thank-you to the authors, publishers, and other copyright holders who gave her permission to quote from their works in this book. We are deeply grateful for your generosity.

Every effort was made to trace the ownership of copyrighted materials and obtain permissions to reproduce them. If any material has been used without proper permission, the author would appreciate being notified so that proper credit may be given in future editions.

ABOUT THE AUTHOR

Evelyn K. Rice is the creator of the "Finding Your Soul Mate™" workshops, a dynamic series that each year helps thousands of singles and couples learn how to create and maintain loving, healthy relationships. She is also a highly sought-after lecturer and corporate consultant with a national and international clientele, and is currently at work on her second book, *Addicted to Struggle™*.

Evelyn's broad appeal stems from her deep understanding of relationships and behaviors, drawn from 16 years of working with individuals and companies, combined with an approach that is both spiritual and practical.

As head of her own consulting firm since 1985, Evelyn has been in great demand as a management training consultant for such clients as IBM, TRW, Sprint, Hoechst Celanese, Lipton, U.S. Government, BlueCross BlueShield, the Bank Administration Institute, and numerous financial institutions. She also maintains a busy speaking schedule around the country and has been featured on a number of television and radio programs.

Evelyn lives in Greensboro, North Carolina, with her Soul Mate, Chris.

CONTACT INFORMATION

To order books and audiotapes, to schedule workshops and speaking engagements, and to contact the author:

Evelyn K. Rice

Rice & Associates, Inc.

P.O. Box 38263

Greensboro, North Carolina 27438

Phone: (336) 370-1555

Fax: (336) 370-4730

Email: ekrice@riceassociates.com

Visit us on the Web at:

www.findyoursoulmate.com

www.riceassociates.com

216 pages

ISBN # 0-9711207-0-6

Finding Your Soul Mate™ Handbook

Don't simply settle! You can create the healthy, loving, successful relationship you've always dreamed of by using the tools in the *Finding Your Soul Mate™ Handbook.*

Brimming with rich, warm and wise advice, this step-by-step, practical book takes an enlightened look at the forces that create and maintain Soul Mate relationships. Absorbingly written, this book walks you through a journey of self-awareness, of choosing the ideal partner, and of creating a relationship that fulfills your deepest desires. It's a celebration of love as an exhilarating, lifelong adventure.

Discover what the *Finding Your Soul Mate™ Handbook* has to say about:

- What is a Soul Mate relationship?
- The psychology of why we are attracted to certain people
- Factors that contribute to repeating harmful patterns
- Understanding "is this love or not?"
- How childhood wounds affect your choice of partners
- The three foundational keys for creating a Soul Mate relationship
- The four phases of relationships
- How to begin moving a relationship beyond the "power struggle"
- The seven myths about Soul Mate relationships

384 pages

ISBN # 0-9711207-1-4

Finding Your Soul Mate™ *journal*

The journey to the love and fulfillment of a Soul Mate relationship begins with you. It's a marvelous journey in which you awaken to the person you are and the joy that life has to offer, and it's the key to all that will follow. Evelyn K. Rice's *Finding Your Soul Mate™ Journal* is designed to give you a simple tool to chart this exhilarating time of discovery and growth. Based on the *"Four Rivers of Life"* introspective program developed by Angeles Arrien, it's an easy and enjoyable way to stay awake to your dreams and goals. An ideal companion to the *Finding Your Soul Mate™ Handbook,* it can also be used independently with wonderful results.

Finding Your Soul Mate™ Handbook
and the Companion
Finding Your Soul Mate™ Journal

ORDER FORM

Please complete this form and mail or fax to the address below. Or, go to our web site and order on-line.

Finding Your Soul Mate™ Handbook
_____ copies at $16.95* each...$_____.___

Finding Your Soul Mate™ Journal
_____ copies at $14.95* each...$_____.___

SPECIAL OFFER!
Order *Finding Your Soul Mate™ Handbook & Journal* as a set and SAVE $4.00!
_____ sets at $27.90* each..$_____.___

Great GIFT idea!

Shipping & Handling *(International shipping rates vary, please call or e-mail)*
_____ items at $3.50 first item, $2.50 each additional item....$_____.___
Note: Special Offer set counts as two items for shipping.

Tax
North Carolina residents add 6% sales tax ....$_____.___

TOTAL
Thank you for your order! ....$_____.___

*Payable in U.S. Funds only. Call for quantity discounts.
Orders ship within 5–7 business days upon receipt of order.

Name _____

Address_____

City _____ State _____ Zip _____

Phone ( ) _____ E-mail _____

❏ MasterCard ❏ VISA ❏ Discover ❏ American Express

Card # _____Exp.____/ _____

Card Holder's Signature _____

Rice & Associates, Inc.
P.O. Box 38263 • Greensboro, North Carolina 27438
Phone: (336) 370-1555 • Fax: (336) 370-4730

www.findyoursoulmate.com • ekrice@riceassociates.com